0075828

KT-486-214

RAF
(gra)

ISSUES IN POLITICAL THEORY

Series editors: PETER JONES and ALBERT WEALE

Published

Christopher J. Berry: **Human Nature**
Tom Campbell: **Justice**
Tim Gray: **Freedom**
Michael Lessnoff: **Social Contract**
Richard Lindley: **Autonomy**
Susan Mendus: **Toleration and the Limits of Liberalism**
Andrew Reeve: **Property**

Forthcoming

David Beetham: **Legitimacy**
John Horton: **Political Obligation**
Peter Jones: **Rights**
Raymond Plant: **Equality**
Hillel Steiner: **Utilitarianism**

Series Standing Order

If you would like to receive future titles in this series as they
are published, you can make use of our standing order
facility. To place a standing order please contact your
bookseller or, in case of difficulty, write to us at the address
below with your name and address and the name of the
series. Please state with which title you wish to begin your
standing order. (If you live outside the UK we may not have
the rights for your area, in which case we will forward your
order to the publisher concerned.)

Standing Order Service, Macmillan Distribution Ltd,
Houndmills, Basingstoke, Hampshire, RG21 2XS, England

Freedom

Tim Gray

MACMILLAN

Published by
MACMILLAN EDUCATION LTD
Houndmills, Basingstoke, Hampshire RG21 2XS
and London
Companies and representatives
throughout the world

Edited and typeset by Povey/Edmondson
Okehampton and Rochdale, England

Printed in Singapore

British Library Cataloguing in Publication Data
Gray, Tim, 1942–
Freedom.   (Issues in political theory).
1. Freedom
I. Title   II. Series
323.44
ISBN 0–333–39177–2 (hardcover)
ISBN 0–333–39178–0 (paperback)

− 9262 (2) /9.99 .3.92

This book is dedicated to my wife, Anne, whose encouragement has been unwavering as always, in the face of considerable personal strain

Contents

Acknowledgements

This book would never have seen the light of day without the help and support of the editors, Peter Jones and Albert Weale. I owe a particular debt to Peter Jones for his detailed and searching comments on earlier drafts, as a result of which many of the arguments in the text have been much improved. I am grateful also to colleagues and friends who attended seminars I gave here at Newcastle University and at the University of York on issues of freedom, and to Hillel Steiner for his helpful comments on Chapter 4. I would like to acknowledge the stimulus given to my interest in the concept of freedom by many undergraduate students who have taken my political thought course during the last twenty-five years, particularly those who opted for a special subject in liberty, most notably Kate Saxton, and I am especially grateful to Ian Carter, now a postgraduate student, for his generous assistance in helping me to understand some of the problems connected with the measurement and distribution of freedom. Finally, my thanks are due to the University of Newcastle Upon Tyne for granting me two terms of study leave in order to complete the writing.

Department of Politics   *Tim Gray*
University of Newcastle upon Tyne

Introduction

The concept of freedom has attracted more attention than any other concept in the history of political thought. This is because of its popularity and its ambiguity. Its popularity is obvious; from the Ancient Greeks to the present day, politicians, religious leaders and philosophers have vied with one another to yoke liberty firmly to their particular banner, creed or cause. It is an all too familiar fact that political parties everywhere in the modern world claim that one of their principal objectives is freedom. Moreover, outside the constitutional arena we frequently encounter references to 'freedom fighters' and 'liberation movements', testifying to the 'degree to which freedom has become the central value of our culture' (Taylor, [C], 1984, p.100). Clearly, the reason why so many different political parties and movements *choose* to use the language of freedom is because the concept of liberty generally evokes favourable images in the mind of the populace. The reason why they are *able* to present their very different policies in terms of freedom is because the concept of liberty is ambiguous; there are literally hundreds of definitions of freedom, and it is not difficult for a political party to select a definition that fits in closely with its particular policy profile. As a result, a great variety of different programmes are enunciated in the name of freedom. The question arises, however, whether the notion of freedom is thereby being stretched too far – whether liberties are being taken with the concept of liberty – whether, in John Gray's words, 'when these writers use the same word, "liberty" or "freedom", they are using it to mean such different things – that...their reflections lack any common subject matter.' (Gray, 1984, p.1).

It is the purpose of the first two chapters of this book to answer this question, by exploring the nature of the concept of liberty in order to show both what is the core meaning common to all its usages (Chapter 1), and what is the central range of interpretations of that core meaning (Chapter 2). It will be argued in Chapter 1,

1

after a preliminary discussion of whether freedom is an inherently value-laden notion, that Berlin is wrong to claim that there are two competing concepts of liberty (negative and positive), and that MacCallum is right to claim that there is only one concept (that embodied in the triadic formula that 'X is free from Y to do or be Z'). Nevertheless, different interpretations of the X, Y, and Z factors within that formula yield quite distinct conceptions of the concept of liberty, and it is the purpose of Chapter 2 to explore the seven most important such conceptions. Roughly speaking, the first four are conceptions of *interpersonal or social* freedom, while the last three are conceptions of *intrapersonal or psychological* freedom. In the succeeding three chapters, an attempt will be made to clarify the most important remaining issues which are raised by the concept of liberty. Chapter 3 critically examines an assumption which is often taken for granted – that liberty is valuable. In exploring the issue of how freedom is to be justified, we will find that while none of the six justificatory arguments considered succeeds in justifying freedom *simpliciter* (indeed few of them are designed to do so), many of them provide substantiation for particular liberties in certain contexts. Chapter 4 addresses the thorny problem of how, if at all, liberty can be measured. Can we quantify units of freedom, or are liberties incommensurate? Are there degrees of freedom reflecting grades of importance of actions, and rates of difficulty in performing them? These are issues of acute contemporary significance, since nowadays international league tables of human rights protection and violation are perpetually being drawn up and apparently used in foreign policy formulation. Finally, Chapter 5 discusses the related issues of the aggregation and distribution of freedom in societies – in particular, whether its net extent can be increased, or whether the amount of liberty in a society is always fixed, entailing that only its distribution can be varied; and whether we should aim to maximise the sum of freedom in society, or to equalise everyone's holdings of it. An attempt is made in this chapter to orient the discussion towards public policy, by examining aggregative and distributive issues within the context of debates over the institution of private property. This is partly to provide a concrete and practical feel to the discussion, but also because it is over the ownership and distribution of private property that much of the current controversy surrounding aggregative and distributive issues of freedom ranges.

1 The Meaning of Freedom

Attempting to make sense of the bewildering variety of definitions of freedom is a daunting task. I propose to do so by firstly, in this chapter, examining what kind of concept the notion of liberty is – i.e. is it a value-free or a value-laden concept?; is it a single concept or are there two concepts? From this examination I will conclude that while there is only one *concept* of liberty – a value-free definition acceptable to all parties – there are many *conceptions* of that single concept of liberty – all of which are value-laden in character. Secondly, in Chapter 2, I consider the seven most prominent of these conceptions of the concept of liberty.

There is one preliminary issue to be quickly resolved: is 'liberty' synonymous with 'freedom'? Some writers have suggested that they are different concepts. For example, Dybikowski (1981, pp.339–40) has argued that 'liberty' is an attribute of agents, while 'freedom' is an attribute of inanimate things. Belaief (1979, p.127) claims that 'freedom relates to the metaphysical nature of the self...liberty relates to the social or political dimension'. A more sustained attempt to distinguish between liberty and freedom has been made by Pitkin. Drawing on Arendt's view that 'liberties' imply protection from state interference, whereas 'freedom' implies active involvement in politics, Pitkin (1988, pp.542–3) suggests that 'liberty' is more 'plural and piecemeal', whereas 'freedom' is 'more likely to be holistic, to mean a total condition or state of being'. Also, 'liberty' is more external, whereas 'freedom' is more 'psychic, inner, and integral to the self'; 'liberty' operates more on 'the rational surface of things', whereas 'freedom' generates more philosophical puzzles.

However, there is no conceptual distinction demonstrated here, only a distinction of style – an assertion of linguistic preference or convenience. The fact that we find it more felicitous, for example, to use the word 'liberty' than the word 'freedom' when referring to 'civil liberty', and to use the word 'freedom' rather than the word

'liberty' when referring to 'freedom of the will', in no way entails
that 'liberty' is a political concept, or that 'freedom' is a
metaphysical concept. It would only be a stylistic idiosyncrasy,
not a conceptual error, to refer to 'civil freedom' or to 'liberty of the
will' (as Hobbes does). The substitution of the one word for the
other might render certain sentences less conventional, but it would
not alter their essential meaning (Cranston, 1967, p.32).

1 A value-free or a value-laden concept?

A more difficult and important issue is whether liberty can be
defined entirely in value-free (i.e. descriptive or empirical) terms, or
whether it is a value-laden (i.e. prescriptive or normative) concept. Is
liberty a notion like oxygen, that everyone can agree has a standard,
objective meaning? Or is liberty a notion like happiness, that
necessarily embodies and reflects the different values held by
different people, thereby precluding any hope of general agreement
on its meaning? The view that freedom can be defined entirely in
value-free terms has been put forward by several writers, notably
Steiner (1974/5, p.35) and Oppenheim (1962, p.275). On this view,
the statement that X is free from Y to do Z is not a value judgement,
but an empirical statement, and as such it can be accepted by
everyone, irrespective of their differing value-systems or ideological
convictions. Accordingly, there is always, in principle, a single right
answer to the question of whether someone is free to do something.
Unless freedom can be defined in value-free terms, so the argument
runs, it is difficult to see how we could ever make meaningful
comparisons between the freedom of one person and another, or
between one country and another, since without an agreed definition
of liberty, we would not be comparing like with like.

Nevertheless, the claim that it is possible to have a value-free
definition of freedom has been much criticised. The critics argue that
all definitions of liberty are value-dependent, since values inevitably
figure in the criteria by which liberty is identified. A simple respect
in which liberty is said to be value-laden is the fact that the terms
'liberty', 'freedom', 'free' are always used in an approbatory sense,
indicating approval, and never in a pejorative sense, indicating
disapproval. For example, we are said to be free from taxes, but not
from dividends (Cranston, 1967, p.4). The positive aura of freedom

is also evident in the deprecatory expressions that we commonly employ to denote a condition of unfreedom, such as 'interference' and 'coercion'. So the term 'freedom' or its synonym is restricted to those actions of which we approve, and the term 'unfreedom' or its synonym is used to denote those actions of which we disapprove. Hence the definition of freedom is necessarily value-laden.

This attempt to show how liberty is value-dependent is, however, unconvincing. Not all usages of the term 'freedom' are approbatory; for example, the terms 'free love', 'free thinking', and even 'free enterprise' are often used pejoratively (Cranston, 1967, pp.11–12), while not all usages of the term 'unfreedom' are disapprobatory; for example, we approve of forms of coercion such as those employed by parents, teachers and the police. The truth is, as we will argue in Chapter 3, freedom is neither good nor bad in itself: whether it is good or bad depends upon the use to which it is put (Somerville, 1962, p.289).

A more convincing attempt to show that liberty is a value-laden concept is the claim that value-judgements intrude whenever we attempt to conceptualise freedom. For example, Bronaugh (1963/4, pp.163–72) argues that, when we say that a person is unfree because he had no choice, we are making an evaluative judgement about whether or not that person could reasonably have been expected to act differently in the circumstances in which he found himself. Miller (1983/4, p.67) argues that, when we say that Y restricts X's freedom, we are making an evaluative judgement that Y bears moral responsibility for the restriction. Benn and Weinstein (1971, p.195) argue that when we say that X is free to do Z, we are making an evaluative judgement that Z is something that a rational agent could consider doing.

The argument here is that any substantive statement about freedom contains within it, either implicitly or explicitly, some controversial value-judgement. We may not accept the explanations of Bronaugh, Miller or Benn and Weinstein as to the particular form which these value-judgements take, but it does seem undeniable that freedom statements are evaluative in some way(s). In other words, there does seem to be an element of 'essential contestability' about freedom. Gallie, in a seminal article, first drew attention to the notion of essential contestability, pointing out that there are some concepts, 'the proper use of which inevitably involves endless disputes about their proper uses on the part of their users' (Gallie,

1955/6, p.169). For example, the concept of democracy has at least three distinct meanings; (i) 'the power of the majority of citizens to choose (and remove) governments'; (ii) 'equality of all citizens ... to attain to positions of political leadership and responsibility'; (iii) 'active participation of citizens in political life' (Gallie, 1955/6, pp.184–5). The dispute between the respective advocates as to which one of these interpretations represents the essence of the concept of democracy may not be resolvable. This is not to deny that debates concerning the different meanings of a concept such as democracy can be conducted in a rational manner, or that they may result in changes of mind among the debaters. But in the end, different views about an essentially contested concept are based upon 'fundamental differences of attitude, of a kind for which no logical justification can be given' (Gallie, 1955/6, p.191).

However, there must be *some* common ground between the opposed views, since unless there is agreement on what it is that the disputants are disagreeing about, the controversy is not a substantive one, but simply a debate about words. (Hancock, 1962, p.645). Gallie expresses this as the need for an 'exemplar' of the concept, on which all the parties are agreed, disagreement being confined to different interpretations of what that exemplar entails. In the case of the concept of democracy, for example, the exemplar is derived from 'a long tradition ... of demands, aspirations, revolts and reforms of a common *anti-in*egalitarian character' (Gallie, 1955/6, p.186). Swanton (1984/5, p.816), however, has argued that the so-called conceptual common core of a concept such as liberty is itself value-laden. Indeed, it might be argued that to demand an exemplar undermines the thesis of essential contestability, in that it suggests that underlying all the disputes over a concept, one fundamentally uncontested element exists – its common core.

My view is that Gallie and others are right to distinguish between the common core of a concept and its varying interpretations, and to confine controversy to the latter, since unless there is some acknowledged common ground, meaningful disagreement seems impossible. Putting this in terms of the discussion to come, there is only one *concept* of liberty, but there are many *conceptions* of that concept. Essential-contestedness is confined to different conceptions of freedom; it does not extend to the basic core meaning of the concept of liberty itself. Accordingly, on the issue of whether liberty is a value-free or a value-laden concept, my conclusion is that it may be *defined* in value-free terms (this definition constitutes the concept of freedom), but that any *interpretation* of that definition is value-laden (these interpretations constitute the conceptions of freedom). The questions concerning the meaning of freedom that remain to be answered are: first, what is the nature of this value-free definition or concept of freedom?; and second, what are the divergent interpretations of that definition, i.e. the conceptions of that concept? The first question forms the focus for the remainder of this chapter, and the second question is answered in Chapter 2.

2 Two concepts of liberty or only one?

The conclusion I reached above – that there is only one concept of liberty but many conceptions of that single concept – is rejected by Berlin, who argues that there are two concepts of liberty, the negative and the positive. In what follows, I examine Berlin's argument, and conclude that he is mistaken in his view that the controversies surrounding liberty are to be understood fundamentally in terms of a basic opposition between two alternative concepts of freedom. I follow MacCallum in arguing that there is only one concept of freedom, which is encapsulated in the triadic formula that 'X is free from Y to do or be Z'. I examine Berlin's position first.

(a) Berlin's two concepts of liberty

Berlin was not the first (or the last) to distinguish between a 'negative' and a 'positive' concept of liberty. Indeed, that distinction in one form or another has been implicit, if not always explicit, in political thought since the Ancient Greeks. Berlin's contribution was to elaborate the distinction to such an extent that it has now become part of the staple fare of every analysis of freedom. The negative sense is, Berlin says, involved in the question 'What is the area within which the subject – a person or group of persons – is or should be left to do or be what he is able to do or be, without interference by other persons?'. The positive sense is, he says, involved in the question 'What, or who, is the source of control or interference that can determine someone to do, or be, this rather than that?' (Berlin, 1969, pp.121–2). Whereas the negative concept is concerned with the *area* of control, the positive concept is concerned with its *source*. What matters for the negative concept is not 'who rules me?', but 'how many rules restrict my actions?' Hence negative freedom is compatible with autocracy, provided the autocrat limits the extent of his or her interference. What matters for the positive concept is not the area of non-interference, but the fact of self-government. Hence positive freedom is compatible with extensive constraint, provided it is self-imposed. At their root, these two concepts of freedom – area of non-interference and self-government – may not seem very far apart; 'no more than negative and positive ways of saying much the same thing'. But their conceptual differences emerged as they 'historically developed in divergent directions... until, in the end, they came into direct conflict with each other'. (1969, pp.131–2). What Berlin means by this claim is that the positive concept evolved in such a way as to become the diametrical opposite of the negative concept. From the notion of self-government, it was a short step to the claim that the 'self' in question is not the 'actual' self, but the 'real' or 'rational' self; and another short step to the conclusion that in imposing their 'real' self upon their 'actual' self, we can 'force people to be free'.

Berlin's argument is, however, deeply flawed. In the first place, his quasi-historical attempt to show how the two concepts are diametrically opposed to one another fails. Berlin himself admits that there is nothing inherent in the positive concept of freedom that entails a justification for coercion in the name of liberty – the negative concept could equally well have been used to justify tyranny if the distinction between the 'real' and the 'actual' self had been employed in its case (1969, p.xliv) – it is just that 'as a matter of history' the positive concept 'lent itself more easily to this splitting of personality into two' (1969, p.134). But if there is nothing inherently more plausible about deriving the notion of a divided self from the positive rather than from the negative concept of liberty, what is philosophically significant about the alleged historical evolution of the positive concept?

The second weakness in Berlin's analysis is that not only does he fail to show convincingly how the two concepts are diametrically opposed to one another, he fails to demonstrate why the terms 'negative' and 'positive' are employed to distinguish between two meanings of freedom. One reason for employing the terms might be to signify the well-known contrast between 'freedom from' (negative liberty) and 'freedom to' (positive liberty) (1969, pp.127–31). But these labels are quite unhelpful, since virtually any kind of liberty could be expressed in terms of *either* 'freedom from' *or* 'freedom to'. For example, the negative liberty of 'freedom from' restrictions on secondary picketing could be expressed in terms of 'freedom to' picket. As Feinberg (1980, p.5) puts it, 'freedom from' and 'freedom to' are 'two sides of the same coin, each involved with the other, and not two radically distinct kinds of freedom'. Indeed, as we shall see, MacCallum shows that every freedom is simultaneously both *from* something, *to* do something, in that every freedom may be expressed in the form '*X* is free from *Y* to do or be *Z*'.

The terms 'negative' and 'positive' are unhelpful for another reason – they fail to capture the contrast that Berlin is attempting to draw between the area and the source of control. There is nothing particularly 'negative' about the area of a person's freedom from control; and there is nothing particularly 'positive' about the source of control over a person. Moreover, the terms 'negative' and 'positive' freedom are often used by other writers (and sometimes by Berlin himself) to signify a quite different contrast. For example, a very popular interpretation is to associate negative freedom with a *laissez-faire* view of governmental responsibilities (leaving people alone), and to associate positive freedom with an interventionist state (providing people with opportunities). While 'leaving people alone' is connected to the area of control, 'providing people with opportunities' is not at all connected to the source of control. Another common interpretation of the negative/positive dichotomy is to associate the negative concept with social or interpersonal freedom, and to associate the positive concept with psychological or intrapersonal freedom. On this view, negative liberty is freedom from external or physical impediments, and positive liberty is freedom from internal or mental impediments. The contrast between interpersonal and intrapersonal freedom is a helpful one in analysing liberty, and I myself make use of it. But it is not the same as Berlin's contrast between negative and positive liberty. Whereas Berlin's distinction is between the area and the source of control, the distinction between interpersonal and intrapersonal freedom is between two different sets of interpretations of *both the area and the source of control*, one external and the other internal. This is a distinction between different *conceptions*, not *concepts*, of freedom.

Sometimes the distinction between 'negative' and 'positive' liberty has been taken to mean that the negative concept is the value-free notion of freedom, and the positive concept is the value-laden notion of freedom; for instance, negative freedom signifying mere action, and positive freedom signifying action that arises from rational choice or moral decision. This usage has little or no connection with Berlin's distinction between the area and the source of control.

Berlin himself sometimes associates the negative concept (admiringly) with a neutral, tolerant and pluralistic view of society, and the positive concept (disparagingly) with a rationalistic, *dirigiste* and monistic view of society. Indeed, at times, his view of the negative concept is so laudatory, and his view of the positive concept so jaundiced, as to suggest that he regards the former as the only true concept, and the latter as a spurious concept of freedom, of purely metaphorical significance (1969, p.lvi). Such a view threatens to undermine the contrast Berlin is at such pains to draw between two *legitimate* concepts of liberty.

Clearly, then, there is a considerable degree of ambiguity in the terms 'negative' and 'positive' when applied to the concept of freedom. Berlin's own various (and not always consistent) interpretations have no particular priority, but are merely to be counted among a number of confusingly competing usages. A more fruitful way of understanding the notion of freedom is to abandon Berlin's idea that there are different *concepts* of liberty – and to accept instead MacCallum's idea that there is only *one concept* of liberty, and at the same time to recognise that there are a number of different *conceptions* of liberty, which Berlin vainly tried to polarise into two categories, but which stand on their own as alternative explanations of agents, obstacles and objectives (MacCallum's *X*, *Y* and *Z* factors). I will examine MacCallum's argument for a single concept of liberty in the next section of this chapter; and I will consider the main conceptions of liberty in Chapter 2. But first I want to explain the distinction I am drawing here between a *concept* and a *conception*. It is a familiar distinction in political theory, performing a function similar to that served by Gallie's idea of the exemplar of a concept, which incorporates a common core on which all the parties can be agreed while disagreeing over the proper interpretation of that common core. Rawls (1972, pp.5–6) distinguishes between 'the concept of justice' and 'the various conceptions of justice'. The concept of justice is a formal principle requiring that people should be treated equitably and judiciously; everyone can agree on it, while differing over the proper criteria of equity and judiciousness. Dworkin ([R.], 1978, pp.134–5) makes a similar distinction between 'the *concept* of fairness' and 'any specific *conception* of fairness'. The concept of fairness is invoked whenever we say we should treat people fairly; a conception of fairness is invoked whenever we try to interpret what it means to treat people fairly. Waldron (1988, pp.51–2) likewise distinguishes between the concept of private property (represented by 'the idea of ownership') and various conceptions of that concept (represented by 'the detailed rules of particular systems of private property'). Lindley (1986, p.3) argues along the same lines in relation to the concepts of democracy and autonomy, and Lukes (1974, pp.26–7) says much the same about power.

John Gray controversially claims that Berlin himself distinguishes between the concept and the conceptions of liberty. That is to say, Gray (1980, pp.510–25) argues that what Berlin really meant was that negative and positive freedom were not two different *concepts* of liberty, but two different *conceptions* of the *one concept* of liberty. But while it is true that Berlin refers to a shared idea of 'holding off of something or someone' (1969, p.158), it is also true that he denies emphatically that people who champion negative and positive freedom merely hold different views of the same concept. 'The former want to curb authority as such. The latter want it placed in their own hands. That is a cardinal issue. These are not two different interpretations of a single concept, but two profoundly divergent and irreconcilable attitudes to the ends of life' (1969, p.166).

(b) MacCallum's triadic concept of liberty

Despite its shortcomings, Berlin's 'Two Concepts of Liberty', first published in 1958, was a landmark in the history of attempts to elucidate the meaning of freedom – 'a minor classic of modern political theory' as Macfarlane (1966, p.77) put it. MacCallum's article, 'Negative and Positive Freedom', published nine years later, was a second landmark, at least as important as the first, since it clarified once and for all the precise formal meaning of the concept of liberty. MacCallum shows how a genuine statement about freedom always contains three elements: freedom is always

(i) *of* something (the agent); (ii) *from* something (the constraint); (iii) *to* do or be something (the objective). The meaning of freedom is therefore contained in the triadic formula X is free from Y to do or be Z. An illustration may help to bring out the point of MacCallum's triadic formula. If I am asked whether X is free to do Z, say to libel someone, the answer must make reference to the Y factor – i.e. to the obstacles that might prevent X from doing Z. X may be free from some obstacles (such as physical impediments) to do Z, but not free from other obstacles (such as legal restrictions) to do Z. Similarly, if I am asked whether X is free from Y, say legal restrictions, the answer must make reference to the Z factor – i.e. to the objectives pursued by X which legal restrictions may frustrate. X may be free from legal restrictions to make a political speech, but not free from legal restrictions to libel someone.

Where any of these three factors is missing, as in the statements 'X is free from Y', and 'X is free to do Z', MacCallum argues that either the statement is not a genuine statement about freedom, or that the missing factor is implicit and can be inferred from the context in which the statement is uttered. An example of a non-genuine statement about liberty is 'the sky is free of clouds'; here there is no explicit Z factor, nor is it implicit or inferrable from the context, since the X factor (the sky) is incapable of having an objective. The X factor is not an agent, properly so-called, and therefore the word 'free' merely signifies 'without' or 'rid of'. An example of a genuine freedom statement in which one (or two) of the three factors is suppressed is, 'free beer'. Unpacked, this statement refers to 'beer that *people* are free *from* the ordinary restrictions of the market place *to* drink without paying for it' (MacCallum 1967, p.316).

MacCallum argues that this is the only concept of freedom, and that differences of opinion over liberty turn on different interpretations of what (for the purposes of freedom) counts as an agent, a constraint, or an objective. For example, if we consider the first factor, X, the agent, we will find that a difference of opinion between exponents of so-called 'negative' and 'positive' freedom is not about liberty, but about agency. Whereas 'negative' libertarians habitually interpret the agent in terms of the actual or empirical self, 'positive' libertarians sometimes interpret the agent in terms of the 'real' or 'rational' or 'moral' or 'true' self, which may be embodied in institutions or whole communities. Similarly if we consider the second factor, Y, the constraint: exponents of 'negative' freedom generally count as constraints only those impediments which have been imposed upon an agent by other human beings. But some exponents of 'positive' freedom include internal or psychological impediments as constraints on an agent's freedom. Finally, the third factor, *Z*, the objective: 'negative' libertarians usually characterise the objective as some action, whereas 'positive' libertarians often regard the objective as some state of mind or character. In all such controversies, says MacCallum, the real issue is not over what *freedom* is, but over what is to count as an *agent* or *constraint* or *objective* for purposes of freedom.

The triadic interpretation of liberty has been endorsed by many writers, including Benn and Weinstein (1971, p.194), Rawls (1972, p.202), Bayles (1972, p.24), Blackstone (1973, pp.423–4), Feinberg (1980, pp.3–4), and Goodin (1982, p.152). In emphasising the relational character of freedom – i.e. showing that issues of liberty are not raised in absolute terms (is *X* free?), but only in relative terms (what is *X* free from, to do?) – it constitutes the model to which all genuine statements of freedom must conform, and serves as the formal definition of the one and only concept of freedom – a definition that is value-free and can be accepted by all parties whatever their moral and political opinions.

However, these claims on behalf of the triadic concept of freedom have not gone unchallenged. One challenge takes the form of denying the claim that all genuine statements about freedom must contain the third of the three factors that make up the triad – the *Z* factor, the objective. For example, it is suggested by Berlin (1969, p.xliii) that someone may want to be free from chains, or a group of people may want to be free from enslavement, without aiming at any particular objective. Just as someone who has arthritis might want simply to be released from pain, so someone who is unfree might want simply to be released from restriction. Gray (1980, p.511) argues that this means that 'freedom must be regarded as basically a dyadic rather than as a triadic concept'. However, it could be argued that, unlike the arthritic, for whom release from pain may (or may not) be an end in itself, the enchained person wants to be free not as an end in itself, but in order to be in a position to choose for himself to do or not do things (Skinner, [Q.], 1984, p.194). In other words, the *Z* factor or objective is a condition of self-determination.

Another challenge to the triadic formula is, however, more serious. This is the charge that the formula does not, as MacCallum appears to claim it does, eliminate conceptual issues in relation to liberty, but simply displaces or conceals them as conceptual issues about what constitutes an X or Y or Z factor. The fact that the triadic formula focuses our attention exclusively upon disagreements over the X, Y, and Z factors does not mean that conceptual disputes about the nature of liberty itself have disappeared. It may (and does) mean that disputes over the nature of freedom as a *concept* have ended, but it may not (and does not) mean that disputes over *conceptions* of freedom have ended. On the contrary, disagreements about what constitutes an X or Y or Z factor are themselves subsumed forms of disputation about the nature of liberty. MacCallum's claim that it is possible (and necessary) to separate issues of 'what is freedom' from issues of 'what is an agent, a constraint, or an objective', faces the difficulty that the two sets of issues are inextricably entwined together. For example, the issue of what constitutes an agent, raises the question of whether some mentally-ill persons can be regarded as agents. Writers who deem all mentally-ill persons to be agents, do so because they conceive of agency in terms of the capacity for physical movement; writers who deny that some mentally-ill persons can be agents do so because they conceive of agency in terms of the capacity for rational choice. But such conceptions of agency reflect prior conceptions of what freedom itself is (respectively, unimpeded motion and rational decision-making). The writers have framed their definitions of agency in terms which express their conception of freedom. Why, then, should we assume that issues of freedom are resolvable into issues of agency, rather than the other way round? Which comes first, the notion of agency or the conception of freedom? Similarly, our conception of a constraint is inseparable from our conception of freedom. If we conceive freedom in terms of unimpeded motion, we will not regard a neurosis as a psychological constraint on freedom; but if we view freedom in terms of rational decision-making, we will regard a neurosis as a constraint on freedom. Finally, the notion of what constitutes an objective presupposes a conception of freedom. For someone who interprets liberty as unimpeded motion, pursuit of a fantasy is a valid objective; whereas for someone who interprets liberty as rational decision-making, a fantasaical aim could not form part of what is meant by an objective.

The charge here against MacCallum, then, is that before we can begin to discuss intelligibly what are X, Y and Z factors, we need to be clear as to what our conception of freedom is. The debates about the term variables are transposed forms of the debates about the nature of liberty itself. Hence, MacCallum has not eliminated all conceptual controversy about freedom; on the contrary, the essential contestability of freedom as *conception*, though not as *concept*, is confirmed rather than removed by the essential contestability of the term-variables (Gray, 1980, p.511). The triadic formula does not demonstrate that liberty is not an essentially contested or value-laden conception, but only serves to focus attention on the chief areas of contestability – i.e. not the formal value-free triadic concept of freedom, but the unresolvable value-laden disputes about each of the X, Y, and Z factors within the triadic formula, which in turn mirror unresolvable value-laden disputes about liberty as a conception. Indeed, Weale (1983a, p.51) argues that MacCallum's triadic analysis 'does not in fact offer us a definition of liberty or freedom, but simply a specification of the form of sentences about freedom with which an adequate definition should be consistent'.

Conclusion on the meaning of freedom

What, then, are we to conclude? Is liberty a value-free or a value-laden concept? Is there one concept of liberty or two? My view is that MacCallum has demonstrated conclusively that the *formal* meaning of liberty is expressed in terms of the value-free formula that X is free from Y to do or be Z; in this sense there is only one concept of liberty. But he has not shown that there is no real controversy over the *substantive* meaning of different conceptions of liberty; debates about the term-variables of the triadic concept of liberty are themselves debates about the substantive meaning of conceptions of liberty. However, Berlin's theory that debates about the substantive meaning of liberty take the form of a controversy between two opposed views as to what is the correct concept of liberty, is even more misconceived. The truth is that substantive debates (value-laden controversies) concerning conceptions of liberty do not undermine MacCallum's claim that there is only one concept of liberty – the formal (value-free) triadic definition of liberty – but they do indicate that any attempt to interpret or apply that definition is necessarily controversial. There is but one single concept of liberty – the formal meaning of freedom expressed in the value-free terms of MacCallum's triadic formula – but many conceptions of that concept – the substantive meaning of freedom expressed in the value-laden terms of alternative conceptions of that single concept.

2 Conceptions of Freedom

In Chapter 1, I have argued that there is only one *concept* of liberty –
that established by MacCallum in his triadic formula, '*X* is free from
Y to do or be *Z*' – but many *conceptions* of that single concept of
liberty. In this chapter, I wish to examine the seven most prominent
conceptions. But, first, a word to explain why it is important to
identify and discuss these seven conceptions. Subscribing to a
conception of freedom is not simply a semantic exercise; it is also an
expression of the holder's view of human nature and social
relationships. Although freedom may not be the most fundamental
concept in the vocabulary of political theorists, it is nevertheless a
notion of such basic importance to a philosopher's view of the
world, that it is bound to be coloured by his or her value-system.

The first four conceptions – absence of impediments, availability
of choices, effective power and status – may be said to express
different views of social relationships, while the remaining three
conceptions – self-determination, doing what one wants and self-
mastery – may be said to express different views of human nature.
This division of the seven conceptions should not be confused with
Berlin's distinction between negative and positive concepts of
liberty. All seven conceptions lie within a single concept of liberty,
each of them entailing notions of *both* the area of non-interference
(Berlin's 'negative' liberty), *and* the source of control (Berlin's
'positive' liberty). The division between the four interpersonal and
the three intrapersonal conceptions is, therefore, not a difference of
opinion as to whether freedom is bound up with the area or with the
source of control, but a difference of interpretation as to what
constitutes *both* the area of non-interference and the *source* of
control. Moreover, the division between interpersonal and
intrapersonal concepts is not complete; any theory of society is
bound to entail a view of human nature, and any theory of human
nature is bound to entail a view of society. Hence, we will find both

that there are important psychological elements in each of the interpersonal conceptions, and that there are important social elements in each of the intrapersonal conceptions. Nevertheless, the distinction between primarily interpersonal and primarily intrapersonal conceptions of freedom is worth maintaining, if only for heuristic reasons. It will help, for example, in the analysis of questions of measurement, aggregation and distribution of freedom, attempted in Chapters 4 and 5, where, for the most part, the interpersonal conceptions of freedom are used. It will also help us to understand the various conceptions themselves, by identifying a sociological background to the interpersonal conceptions, and a psychological background to the intrapersonal conceptions. Let us look briefly at these respective backgrounds.

Writers who interpret freedom as 'absence of impediments' often view society atomistically, as an aggregate of interacting individual agents whose behaviour impinges upon one another in somewhat mechanical ways. On this view freedom is conceived as holding off other people – preserving one's space and property – creating a sphere of immunity from interference. Writers who interpret freedom as 'availability of choices' frequently hold a consumerist attitude towards society, seeing it in terms of the economic functioning of the market place, where mutual exchange of goods and services is the central feature. Freedom is perceived as the activity of persons engaged in selecting their best options. Writers who interpret freedom as 'effective power', by contrast, generally criticise the market system for its failure to secure more than a formal façade of freedom for the majority of the population. This critique, which may well be based upon a class analysis of capitalism, suggests that governmental intervention to redistribute wealth more equitably is necessary if everyone is to be able to exercise the freedoms otherwise available only to the privileged few. Writers who interpret freedom as 'status' similarly view society in terms of groups rather than as individuals, though, in their case, the emphasis is placed less upon what the members of such groups *do*, than upon what they *are*, as a result of their group membership. Membership of, say, a class or nation confers a sense of social integration, solidarity and involvement, and these are central features of freedom as status.

The three remaining conceptions view freedom more in psychological terms, concentrating attention rather upon the internal workings of agents' minds than upon the external interactions of their bodies. Writers who interpret freedom as 'self-determination' focus upon the issue of free will, in an attempt to discover how far our actions may be said to be independent of causal factors such as heredity or environment. The image of freedom created here is that of the capacity to forge one's own identity, rather than be moulded by forces outside one's control. Writers who interpret freedom as 'doing what one wants' are preoccupied with the nature of people's desires, and this entails an examination of value-systems in order to identify an order of priority between conflicting wants. Freedom as portrayed here is the hedonistic one of desire-satisfaction. Finally, writers who interpret freedom as 'self-mastery' conceive human nature in terms of a divided self, manifesting a struggle between immature elements and mature elements. Freedom consists in mastery by the mature over the immature elements, leading to psychic harmony or peace of mind.

The various pictures of society and human nature drawn here indicate the wider significance of the conceptions of freedom. In selecting particular conceptions of freedom, writers are not simply clarifying a concept, but expressing sharply diverging sociological and psychological views. What these writers are engaged in, therefore, is not merely a debate about words, but a debate about deep philosophical issues concerning the world which we inhabit, and the sort of persons we are.

1 Freedom as absence of impediments

The conception of liberty in terms of the absence of impediments (or interferences, restraints or constraints, etc.) is a familiar one, popularised especially by Hobbes, conveying an image of freedom as unrestricted movement or unobstructed space. On this view, a person is rendered unfree to do something if there is some obstacle standing in the way of her doing it. For example, she is unfree to visit the theatre if she is serving a prison sentence: the locked door of her cell renders her unfree to leave the gaol. The emphasis in this conception of liberty is upon the Y factor, i.e. the fact and nature of the obstacle which serves to deny a person freedom, rather than upon either the X factor (anything can be a free agent on this conception), or the Z factor (less attention is paid to the objective which the agent may be prevented from attaining). As a result, it is a very negative approach to freedom, concerned essentially with what takes liberty away.

This leads us to the first criticism of the absence of impediments conception of freedom, that it defines unfreedom rather than freedom. It tells us what freedom is *not* – freedom is not being impeded – rather than what freedom *is*. As such, it has been described as a 'residual' conception of liberty, an indeterminate entity left over when obstacles to it have been removed. No content is given to the term 'to be free' – it simply means 'to be without something'. Such a meaning may be perfectly legitimate in relation to some uses of the word 'free'. For example, the statement that 'the sky is free of clouds' means that 'the sky is without clouds'. But in relation to other uses, especially those which apply to human beings, the notion of freedom is very poorly characterised as being 'without something'. To make sense of human freedom, some account of the Z factor is required, i.e. what it is that the agent is prevented from doing, not merely an account of the Y factor, i.e. what it is that is impeding the agent. The inadequacy of this view of human freedom is exposed if we consider its logical conclusion; complete freedom would be a condition in which the agent would be spared *all* impediments (Somerville, 1962, p.296). Such a condition would reduce human life to a vacuum or void (Schneider, 1940, p.657). This vacuum would be both environmental and ethical. Flathman (1987, p.148) alludes to its environmental nature by pointing out that many physical, cultural and legal constraints – 'situatedness' – far from restricting freedom, are a prerequisite of freedom. McCloskey (1965, pp.486–7) portrays its ethical nature in terms of the failure of the absence of impediments characterisation to capture the moral grandeur that we commonly associate with freedom. 'If to enjoy liberty is simply to be let alone, i.e. not to be interfered with ... liberty appears as a stunted, sterile thing, rather than as the glorious ideal it is often portrayed as being'.

However, this criticism is unconvincing. The absence of impediments conception of freedom does not reduce freedom to a vacuum or void. The Z factor is not explicit, but it is implicit, in that freedom is interpreted as doing anything that the agent is not prevented from doing. Flathman's point that unless there are some impediments, the very notion of an impediment loses its meaning, is well taken, but it does not entail that freedom cannot mean the absence of impediments. It simply indicates that we do not live in a world in which there can be no impediments. McCloskey's criticism confuses the value of freedom with the fact of freedom.

An alternative way of expressing this criticism is to argue that, in telling us only what unfreedom is (not being impeded), but not what freedom is (how many options we have), it omits an ingredient that is vital if we are to avoid making misleading comparative judgements about freedom. We must calculate not only the extent of a person's unfreedom, but also the extent of her freedom, if we are accurately to measure her total liberty and compare it with that of others. Since I consider the strength of this criticism in the discussion of the availability of choices conception of freedom and in Chapter 4, I will not repeat those evaluations here.

A second criticism of the absence of impediments conception of freedom is that it fails to provide an adequate account of the X factor, the agent. On the absence of impediments view, freedom is merely unobstructed movement. Hence, inanimate objects are free if they are not obstructed. Hobbes argues that a stone rolling down a hill is free. But critics object that this reduces freedom to movement rather than action. The stone moves, but it cannot act, and freedom is a matter of action, not just movement. This is not to deny that physical constraint is the archetypal form of restriction on freedom, but it is so not because it is a restriction on movement, but because it is a restriction on action (Flathman, 1987, p.202).

The upshot of this criticism is that the absence of impediments conception of freedom should be interpreted in terms of actions not movements. This entails, first, that the X factor must be animate, since only animate creatures can perform actions, and, second, that it is only when animate beings are performing actions, not just engaged in movements, that they can be said to be free. Of course, this raises the question of how we are to differentiate an action from a mere movement. For example, is a reflex action an action or merely a movement? Is an habitual action an action or merely a movement? Does action demand deliberation or simply choice? These are important issues to be resolved by both advocates and critics of the absence of impediments conception of freedom. Note, however, that this criticism does not necessarily entail that the agent must be human; nonhuman creatures can perform actions on this view. Of the seven conceptions of freedom, only three of them presuppose that the agent is human – status (though status *could* be attributed to nonhuman animals), self-determination, and self-mastery, since impediments, choice, power and wants are not unique to human beings. Nevertheless, in most accounts of freedom it is taken for granted that the agent is human, and in what follows I will assume that we are referring exclusively to human freedom.

This brings me to the third criticism, which is concerned with the way in which the absence of impediments conception interprets the Y factor, that is to say, its explanation of what is to count as an impediment. At face value, it seems that any obstruction to a person's action is a restriction òn her freedom. But this would entail, for example, that the force of gravity which prevents her from jumping 50 feet into the air, or an avalanche which prevents her from travelling to her destination, reduces a person's freedom. Parent (1974a, p.159) accepts the latter implication; 'Is not the assertion "the blizzard rendered X unfree to continue his travels" perfectly intelligible?' But these implications are resisted by critics such as Berlin and Dryer, who argue that natural obstacles, like the force of gravity and avalanches, reduce our *ability*, not our *freedom*, to do things. Underlying this criticism is the assumption that freedom is an entirely human phenomenon. Just as we take for granted human agency in the X factor, so we are to take for granted human agency in the Y factor; just as we assume that only human beings can be free, so we are to assume that only human beings can impede freedom. I am rendered unfree by an obstacle only if that obstacle is imposed by another person, not if it is the result of an accident of nature.

A somewhat similar analysis could be applied to obstacles that are 'internal', rather than 'external', to the agent. Just as an external obstacle, such as an avalanche, reduces the agent's ability, but not her freedom, to travel, so an internal obstacle, such as a physical handicap, reduces the agent's ability but not her freedom (Dryer, 1964, p.445). The person who is physically disabled is just that: disabled from doing things; she is not unfree to do them (Benn and Weinstein, 1971, pp.197–8). (The complex issues raised by the notion of psychological impediments are dealt with when I consider the self-determination and self-mastery conceptions of freedom.)

However, there are circumstances in which natural obstacles, either internal or external, could be construed as limitations on freedom: where the obstacle in question is removable by human agency. If a natural impediment could be removed by human agency, then the impediment could be interpreted as a restriction on freedom. This raises the issue of acts of omission; human beings may restrict one another's freedom by acts of omission as well as by acts of commission (Wertheimer, 1975, pp.355–60). Failure by someone to remove a natural impediment constitutes a human impediment upon someone's freedom. It may be difficult, however, to determine whether a particular impediment can be removed by human agency, since there are not only physical but practical considerations to be borne in mind. Suppose a natural avalanche could be removed, or a congenital physical disability remedied, only if society devoted its entire resources to snow-clearing or medical research: does society's refusal to remove the obstacle constitute a restriction on the freedom of the traveller or the patient? Blackstone suggests that society must have resources which are sufficient for it to be 'reasonable to expect' it to remove an impediment, before we would deem the impediment to be a restriction on freedom (Blackstone, 1973, p.425). But what is 'reasonable'? I return to this issue in a moment when considering Miller's notion of moral responsibility.

If we are to infer that only human impediments (whether through acts of commission or omission) reduce freedom, we must ask whether all such impediments reduce freedom. This brings us to the question of whether an impediment to action must *prevent* that action in order to render the agent unfree. Parent (1974b, p.433–4) and Steiner (1974/5, p.33) take a hard line on this issue, arguing that the restraint in question must make an action physically impossible if it is to constitute a restriction on freedom. On this view, a legal impediment, which is for many writers the central source of unfreedom, does not render an agent unfree, since she can (physically) perform the illegal act, and take the consequences. Similarly in the case of a threat; a threat may deter, but need not actually prevent, someone from performing an action. In such circumstances the threat would not render the agent unfree. Steiner and Parent adopt their position in order to avoid the view that a person is unfree if she is subjected to any influence which might inhibit her from performing an action. Such a view would entail, as Miller (1983/4 p.75) says, that 'my freedom is impaired by just any decrease in the attractiveness of a contemplated action due to human agency – say the fact that on leaving my room I may run into an obnoxious colleague'. Parent and Steiner claim that any modification of their hard-line position thus plunges us into the subjective area of the perceived undesirability, rather than the objective area of the unfreedom, of actions. It makes freedom dependent upon the particular pattern of each individual's desires, and thereby reduces it to a contingent and subjective notion, whereas the truth is that freedom is a physical fact, not a psychological condition.

The position of Parent and Steiner, that laws and threats in themselves are not restrictions on freedom because they do not physically prevent anyone from doing anything, has been criticised on grounds that we would normally say that if a person is faced with a threat or law which deters her from performing an action, she is unfree to perform that action. Miller gives a telling illustration to support this criticism; compare the situation of a man imprisoned in a ten foot square cage, with a man who is told that if he steps out of a ten foot square which is marked out on the ground he will be shot. On the Parent/Steiner view, only the first man is unfree. But the extent of the two men's confinement is the same; the only difference is the mechanism of that confinement – one is a physical, the other is a psychological mechanism. As Miller (1983/4, p.76) says, 'We may well doubt . . . whether the two cases are different in a way that bears upon our judgements of freedom.' However, if we do judge that such a psychological deterrent removes freedom, how are we to avoid deeming every psychological deterrent (including the risk of bumping into an obnoxious colleague) a restriction on freedom?

Perhaps we might make a distinction between those persons who are actually deterred by a legal sanction or threat from performing an action and those who are not, and judge the former as unfree because they *were* prevented from doing the action, and the latter as free because they were *not* prevented from doing the action? However, such a distinction once again has the counter-intuitive consequence that it makes freedom dependent upon the psychological condition of the agent – as Scott (1959, p.218) acknowledges; 'The people who are especially resistant to threats have the widest freedom'.

The most effective resolution of this conundrum, that threats and laws restrict liberty despite the fact that we are able to defy them, comes from Day and Feinberg. Day (1977, p.259) argues that a person faced with a threat or law forbidding him from performing an action, is unfree, not because he cannot perform the forbidden action or because he may be deterred from doing so, but because he cannot perform it with impunity. That is to say, before the threat or law was issued, he was free to perform the act in question without penalty; but now that the threat or law has been issued, he is no longer able to perform the act without penalty. As Feinberg explains (1980, pp.37–8),

> 'When the highwayman sticks his gun in one's ribs and says "your money or your life", he allows one the option of giving or not giving one's money, and the option of staying or not staying alive, but he closes the option of keeping *both* one's money *and* one's life.'

The Day/Feinberg analysis of the 'your money or your life' threat is more convincing than the Parent/Steiner analysis, according to which the person who succumbs to the gunman's threat has merely altered the pattern of his desires; before the threat was issued, he wanted to keep his money; after the threat was issued, he no longer wanted to keep his money, hence no question of unfreedom is involved (Parent, 1974b, p.434). As Day and Feinberg rightly argue, however, the person threatened has *not* altered the pattern of his desires; he still desires to keep both his money and his life, but he is now prevented from doing so, and must choose between them (Day, 1977, p.258).

Nevertheless, the Day/Feinberg view has been challenged. Miller criticises it for implying that whenever a person can no longer do without penalty what he could do before some human intervention occurred, he is rendered unfree. But there are many circumstances, says Miller (1983/4, p.77), in which people can no longer do what they could do before some human intervention, and yet they remain free. For example, if today I offer to sell my neighbour some tomatoes, whereas in the past I have regularly given them to him for nothing, he cannot now have what he could have in the past, namely both the tomatoes and his money. Yet we would not say he was made unfree.

However, why cannot we accept the implication that such a person was made unfree? Miller argues that, if we did so, we would be extending the boundaries of unfreedom too far. But it may very well be that there are many such ways in which our freedom is restricted; perhaps we ought to adjust our intuitions to recognise these restrictions, rather than deny they are restrictions because they run counter to our intuitions. It is perfectly legitimate to argue that any market transaction which makes it impossible for someone to do without penalty something she could previously do, makes that person unfree in that particular respect (Sterba, 1978, p. 118). The qualifying phrase – 'in that particular respect' – is important, since the fact is that in Miller's example, the neighbour is free in one respect – either to buy or not to buy the tomatoes – but unfree in another respect – to have the tomatoes without paying. The implication of this analysis is that laws and threats, similarly, do not render an agent unfree *simpliciter*; they reduce freedom in one respect – by preventing an agent from performing an act with impunity – but leave the agent free in another respect – to yield or not yield to the sanction. Hence both the Steiner/Parent view and the Day/Feinberg view on laws and threats are correct up to a point: a law or threat leaves me free in one respect (Steiner/Parent), but unfree in another respect (Day/Feinberg).

Whether or not this conclusion is acceptable, there is one qualification of the Day/Feinberg position that seems required. As Steiner points out, it is not the issuing of the threat that prevents a person from doing what she was previously able to do, but the carrying out of that threat. If a hollow threat is issued, then the threatenee's liberty is not reduced, since she is not prevented from doing anything that she could do before the threat was issued (though she may *think* she is so prevented). Day (1977, p.269) has responded to this objection by accepting Steiner's point and adjusting his analysis to accommodate it: only genuine threats constitute an abridgement of liberty. But to take account of situations in which a hollow threat is believed to be genuine, we might interpret the distinction between the issuing and the executing of a threat or law, as a distinction between something that makes people *feel* unfree (the issuing), and something that makes people *be* unfree (the executing).

It is important to note that on the Day/Feinberg analysis, the degree of irresistibility of threats or laws is irrelevant to the question of the unfreedom they bring about. A person is unfree if subjected to a threat or law, no matter how trivial the penalty is for non-compliance, since even a minimal penalty renders her unfree to perform the forbidden act with impunity (Day, 1977, p.259). This enables Day rightly to distinguish between threats and laws on the one hand, which are in one respect always impediments to freedom, and bribes, offers and inducements on the other hand, which are never impediments to freedom, no matter how irresistible they happen to be. A bribe or offer which is made to induce a person not to do X does not prevent her from doing X with impunity. Before the bribe was made, she could do X with impunity; after the bribe has been made she can still do X with impunity. Of course she foregoes the offered reward if she does X, but she would also have been without the reward if she did X before the offer was made to her. Hence what she can do after the offer has been made is exactly the same as what she could do before the offer was made.

It is similar with many other kinds of alleged impediments, says Day (1977, p.263), such as advertising and propaganda, which may well influence our behaviour but which do not render us unfree, because they do not prevent us from doing with impunity anything that we could do before we were exposed to them Plamenatz (1968, p.111), however, takes a different view, arguing that X prevents Y from performing an action which Y originally wanted to perform, merely 'by supplying him with a motive for abstaining from it.' But as Dryer (1964, p.446) points out, this would imply that any influence whatsoever that is exerted by X on Y must impair Y's freedom. Such a view would reduce freedom in any society to negligible proportions. Day's account is more convincing, though it does not address the important issue of whether such influences can *determine* human behaviour: this is an issue which will be explored in the examination of the conception of freedom as self-determination.

How does the Day/Feinberg analysis take care of self-imposed constraints? If I impose a constraint upon myself, am I less free as a result? Suppose I have accepted an obligation to attend a party political committee meeting, am I unfree to accept a subsequent invitation to a dinner on the same evening? I am physically free to go to the dinner, but suppose that there are penalties attached to that course of action, such as the threat of ostracism by my fellow party members or even my expulsion from the party. This means that I can not both go to the dinner and avoid a penalty; I can not go to the dinner with impunity. It may seem odd to say that I can make myself unfree – that the X and Y factors are the same person – but it is a perfectly familiar use of language. When someone gets married, for example, we accept that she has taken on certain legal obligations which restrict her future actions; at the very least she can no longer get married legally without first getting divorced.

Day does not, however, apply his analysis in this way. Giving the example of a man who resolves to give up drinking and imposes a duty upon himself to pay £100 to charity whenever he breaks this resolution, Day (1987, p.180) argues that there is no restriction on the man's freedom, because if he 'breaks his rule, he can simply disregard his resolution, and so *can* both break his rule and keep (all of) his money'. This may be true, but suppose the man legally empowers the charity to extract £100 from his bank account every time he starts drinking. In these circumstances his self-imposed constraint would, on Day's analysis, restrict his freedom, since the penalty would have become inescapable. Similarly, in the example of the invitation to dinner, on the assumption that the penalty of ostracism or expulsion is likewise inescapable, I am unfree to go to the dinner. Whether self-imposed constraints do or do not make the agent unfree, therefore, depends upon the inescapability of the penalties involved. Whenever I impose an inescapable sanction upon my conduct, I make myself less free as a result.

However, the Day/Feinberg analysis clarifies our understanding of the absence of impediments conception of freedom only by making use of the assumptions which underlie another conception, that of availability of choices. Day and Feinberg are arguing that the defining characteristic of an impediment to freedom is that it removes an option previously available. They imply, therefore, that the absence of impediments conception of freedom may not stand alone, but depends upon another conception for its elucidation. This is another indication that we cannot deduce from the notion of 'absence of impediments' itself which impediments reduce freedom and which do not; some criterion imported from outside is required to make this distinction.

We must now return to the issue of responsibility mentioned above in connection with the question of whether natural obstacles might be caused or removed by human agency. The issue is this. We have found that to qualify as a restriction on freedom, an impediment must satisfy two conditions: it must be imposed by human means; and it must prevent the agent from doing something with impunity. Are we to add a third condition, that only if the person imposing the impediment does so deliberately, or bears moral responsibility for doing so, is it a restriction on the agent's freedom? There are two distinct notions here which must be separated, the notion of intentionality and the notion of responsibility. Let us take them in turn. First, intentionality. Parent (1974a, p.159) argues that intentionality is irrelevant to the question of freedom: 'a man who has been accidentally locked in his room is as unfree to leave as is someone who has been intentionally locked inside with him'. However, other writers have argued that unless there is an intention to impede on the part of the impeder, the impediment falls into the category of a natural impediment; the person who is unintentionally impeded is made unable, but not unfree, to leave the room, since his incarceration is entirely accidental (Dryer, 1964, pp.445–6; White, 1969/70, p.192).

This is a difficult issue to resolve. Both arguments are persuasive, but each of them entails difficulties. We cannot accept Parent's argument without implying that all natural impediments are restrictions on freedom. We cannot accept Dryer's argument without implying that there are no circumstances in which unintentional impediments can reduce freedom. Miller (1983/4, p.81) suggests a solution, arguing that only those impediments (whether intentional or not) for which moral responsibility can be attributed, are restrictions on freedom. The crucial criterion, then, is moral responsibility, not intentionality (Sterba, 1978, pp.117–18). If a caretaker inadvertently locks someone in a room, then since she bears the moral responsibility for checking that the room was empty before locking up, her action makes that person unfree. The notion of moral responsibility also enables Miller to deal with a problem raised earlier, concerning the fact that many natural obstacles may be removed by human agency, but only at enormous cost to the community. If we were to maintain that all such natural obstacles were impediments to freedom, then this would virtually eliminate the distinction between inability and unfreedom (Miller, 1983/4, p.74). By invoking the notion of moral responsibility, Miller can distinguish between those inabilities which, consistent with its other commitments, it is feasible for society to remove, and those inabilities which it cannot remove, save by abandoning its other commitments. Only the former inabilities count as unfreedoms, since only those are within the moral responsibility of society to remove. However, this solution leaves open the vexed question of what a society's 'other commitments' are, and whether the priorities which these commitments reflect are defensible. Which inabilities we judge to count as unfreedoms, therefore, may well depend upon our ideological position.

Conclusion on the absence of impediments conception of freedom

The conception of freedom in terms of the absence of impediments cannot be accepted in itself as a complete answer to the question of how we are to interpret liberty. Many impediments do not restrict freedom, and the distinction between those impediments which do restrict freedom and those which do not can only be made by going beyond the 'absence of impediments' conception itself and importing a criterion from one of the other conceptions of freedom. The illuminating analysis of Day and Feinberg made use of the conception of freedom in terms of the availability of choices, demanding as a condition of unfreedom that an impediment cuts off a previously available option. But we could make use of one of the other conceptions, defining freedom-reducing impediments as those which inhibit a person's effective power, status, self-determination, 'want-satisfaction or self-mastery. The point is that the absence of impediments conception of freedom is a parasitic conception; it cannot stand convincingly on its own, since for its elucidation we must have recourse to some other conception. On the other hand, there is also a sense in which the other six conceptions are parasitic upon the absence of impediments conception, since underlying them all is an implicit assumption that freedom is restricted by impediments. Impediments which stand in the way of choices, power, status, self-determination, wants or self-mastery make the agent unfree. The truth is that there is a condition of mutual dependence between the first and the subsequent conceptions of freedom. In this sense, the 'absence of impediments' conception of freedom stands as a fundamental constitutive part of our notion of liberty. In terms of MacCallum's analysis it emphasises the fact that a necessary and integral feature of any statement about unfreedom is the presence of some obstacle (the Y factor). But since this fact does not exhaust our understanding of freedom, we must supplement its illumination about the nature of that Y factor with the light thrown by other conceptions upon the nature of the Y factor and also upon the nature of the X and Z factors. Let us now turn to the conception which Day used in interpreting the absence of impediments view – availability of choices.

2 Freedom as availability of choices

The conception of liberty as availability of choices is more positive than the absence of impediments conception, in that it emphasises the presence of something (choice) – the Z factor – rather than the absence of something (impediment) – the Y factor. Moreover, unlike the absence of impediments conception, there is built into the availability of choices conception both the notion that freedom involves action rather than movement (since the exercise of choice is an act of decision making, not merely a motion of the body), and the notion that the subject of freedom must be a creature capable of choosing (thereby excluding both inanimate objects and animate creatures unable to make choices from the sphere of freedom). Benn and Weinstein (1971) have provided the standard account of the availability of choices conception of liberty, according to which, freedom exists in so far as a person has a choice between alternative courses of action, and the more numerous these alternatives are, the greater the liberty. It is an interpretation of liberty which is enjoying considerable popularity in Britain and America today, especially in right-wing political circles.

Elucidation of this conception of freedom raises a number of important issues, four of which relate to the notion of choices (the Z factor), and the remainder of which relate to the notion of a chooser (the X factor). The first issue arises out of the contrast between this conception and that of the absence of impediments. In diametrical contrast to the absence of impediment view of freedom, which tells us what it is to be unfree but not what it is to be free, the availability of choices view tells us what it is to be free, but not what it is to be unfree. We touched upon this point earlier in discussing the absence of impediments view; let us examine it in more detail here. The criticism is that the absence of impediments view tells us how *unfree* we are by counting the number of restrictions upon us, but it cannot tell us how *free* we are, because it only counts restrictions. Conversely, the availability of choices view tells us how *free* we are by counting the number of options open to us, but it cannot tell us how *unfree* we are, because it only counts options. Hence the absence of impediments view ignores one half of the equation, and the availability of choices view ignores the other half. A complete picture of someone's freedom requires both an account of the impediments upon her (what she cannot do), and an account of the

choices open to her (what she can do). If we used either of these
criteria on its own, we would arrive at misleading conclusions when
calculating comparative levels of freedom. For example, since X, an
American citizen, has many more options open to her than Y, a
Robinson Crusoe desert islander, in relation to travel, marriage,
housing, occupation, etc., on the choice criterion we would judge X
to be freer than Y. But if we take into account the fact that there are
fewer legal, social and political impediments on Y than on X, then
we may judge Y to be freer than X.

However, it has been argued that this criticism is misconceived,
because measurement of unfreedom is necessarily also measurement
of freedom, and vice versa. The two conceptions of freedom
calculate the same thing – the extent of freedom – but from opposite
perspectives. The one counts unfreedoms, the other counts
freedoms, but by implication, counting unfreedoms means counting
freedoms and counting freedoms means counting unfreedoms, so
the outcome of the two calculations must be the same. Suppose, for
example, there is a total of 100 actions. Using the absence of
impediments view of freedom, if we calculate that X is prevented
from performing 30 of these actions, then using the availability of
choices view of freedom we must reach the conclusion that X is free
to choose 70 of those actions. On both views, the same conclusion is
reached – that X is unfree to the extent of 30 per cent of possible
actions, and free to the extent of 70 per cent of possible actions.

However, this conclusion depends upon the assumption that
impediments are defined in terms of closing off options – i.e. that
impediments and choices are reciprocal relations of one another, so
that wherever there is an impediment there is a restriction on choice,
and wherever there is a choice there is an absence of impediment.
But such an assumption may not always hold water. Take, for
example, Robinson Crusoe on his desert island; he has no choice of
going to the theatre, but no one has prevented him from doing so.
There may, therefore, be a discrepancy between the extent of
freedom calculated negatively on the impediments scale, and the
extent of freedom calculated positively on the choices scale. (I return
to this issue in Chapter 4.)

The second issue arising out of the availability of choices
conception of freedom concerns the question of which choices are
relevant to freedom. As it stands, the availability of choices
conception would suggest that any and every choice enhances

liberty. But just as we do not regard any and every impediment as relevant to freedom, so we do not regard any and every choice as relevant to freedom. For example, some choices are not, in the nature of things, possible, but we would not say that our freedom was limited as a result. Otherwise, as Fuller (1955, p.1309) puts it, 'a man might be said to be unfree because he does not have the alternative of living forever or being two places at once'.

More controversially, Benn and Weinstein (1974, p.436) claim that what counts as an available option depends on the social context. For example, if it is a standard expectation in a society that everyone is taught to swim, then if X is not taught to swim, X is deprived of freedom; but if there is no such standard expectation, then X is not deprived of freedom. However, this makes freedom a culture-relative conception; what counts as freedom in one society will not count as freedom in another society, simply because the standard expectations differ in the two societies. As a result, the possibility of making meaningful comparisons of the extent of freedom between societies is diminished.

Benn and Weinstein (1971, p.195) also argue that some choices – such as cutting off one's ears – are not relevant to freedom because they are 'bizarre'. Benn (1988, pp.128–9) claims that 'it is incongruous to talk of unfreedom to do things that there could be no point in doing', and gives an example of such an incongruity in the statement that a person is unfree to drink nitric acid. But the reason why we would not normally include in a list of someone's liberties their freedom to cut off their ears or drink nitric acid, is not because they are not freedoms, but because they are freedoms which we take for granted, which go without saying, which do not need to be listed because it would be tedious to do so. Nevertheless, they are liberties.

Norman (1987, p.38) argues that indistinguishable choices are not relevant to freedom, since if there is nothing to choose between options, my freedom is not enhanced by having such options: 'the degree of freedom is determined not by the sheer number of the choices available, but by the range of meaningful choice'. However, what Norman's distinction between indistinguishable and mean-ingful choices is measuring is not freedom, but the value of freedom. The addition of an option which is indistinguishable from an option already available may be of little value to the agent, but it is nonetheless an addition to her freedom. Moreover, it may be a significant part of one's freedom to be able to have options which, though regarded as valueless now, may become important in the future.

Berlin (1969, p.130f) argues that hard choices may not contribute to an agent's freedom; 'not all choices are equally free, or free at all'. For example, 'If in a totalitarian state I betray my friend under threat of torture, perhaps even if I act from fear of losing my job, I can reasonably say that I did not act freely. Nevertheless, I did, of course, make a choice...' Presumably Berlin is not arguing that whenever someone makes a choice under pressure, she is not acting freely. Most choices are made under pressure of some sort; indeed every choice has some opportunity cost attached to it (Benn, 1988, p.142; Benn and Weinstein, 1971, p.198). Freedom of choice does not entail that all choices must be completely costless; indeed, even a threat could be regarded as simply a costly option (Bergmann, 1977, p.73). Strawson (1986, p.396) illustrates this view with the example of the bank clerk who acts freely in choosing to hand over the money to the gangster threatening her with a gun. The element of free choice here (in choosing either to hand over the money or to refuse to do so), is that element mentioned earlier in connection with the interpretation of threats by the absence of impediments conception of freedom – i.e. that although the agent cannot do with impunity what she could previously do, she is still physically free to choose to resist the threat (and take the consequences).

However, Benn and Weinstein (1971, p.209) argue, like Berlin, that if the costs are too high, the choice can no longer be deemed a free one, since it is 'ineligible'. If to a course of action there is attached a penalty that renders it 'ineligible' to the agent, then although the agent *could* (is physically able to) choose it, she is *not free* to choose it. Effectively she has no option.

Apart from the issue of whether or not 'ineligible' simply means 'extremely costly', rather than 'unfreeing', the notion of ineligibility is vulnerable to the charge of ambiguity and imprecision. In what way is an action ineligible to a person? Is there any objective measure of ineligibility, or is the criterion of ineligibility always relative to the individual agent? White (1969/70, pp.196–200) attempts to answer these questions by making a distinction between 'internal' and 'external' ineligibility. Internal ineligibility is psychological in character, and does *not* raise questions of freedom. For example, 'marrying a Negro would not be eligible to a white racist', but since such an option is ineligible only because of the beliefs of the agent, the white racist is not unfree to marry black woman; he is unable to bring himself to do so. External ineligibility is social in character, and *does* raise questions of freedom. For example, 'an employee might be threatened with dismissal if he dresses eccentrically'. However, the distinction drawn by White is not convincing, since both internal and external ineligibility are psychological in character. If the racist is rendered unable rather than unfree by his beliefs, then the employee threatened with dismissal for his eccentric dress is rendered unable rather than unfree by his tastes. Alternatively, if the eccentrically dressed employee is unfree to dress eccentrically, then the racist is also unfree to marry the black. The notion of ineligibility does not therefore seem a convincing way of refuting the view that hard choices are still free choices.

We have considered two of the four issues raised in connection with the notion of choices – that counting choices is a measure of freedom but not of unfreedom, and that some so-called choices may not be genuine choices. The third issue relates to the number of choices; there are circumstances in which increased choice may mean less freedom. Fuller (1955, p.1311) draws attention to the logical extreme of this argument that total freedom of choice would be self-defeating, in that if the individual had 'to choose everything for himself, the burden of choice would become so overwhelming that choice itself would lose its meaning'. He gives the example of language; if we had the option of choosing our own language, we would be at a loss as to how to express ourselves. The complex cultural and institutional framework in which we live and which inevitably restricts our choices, must therefore be seen not as an 'unfortunate limitation' on our liberty, but as 'essential to freedom itself. It preserves us from the suffocating vacuum of free choice into which we would be precipitated if we had to choose everything for ourselves'. However, Fuller's argument can be criticised for confusing the meaning of freedom with the value of freedom. He claims that total freedom of choice would mean that 'choice itself would lose its meaning', but what total freedom of choice actually entails is that choice would lose its *value*, and would become oppressive and burdensome.

A controversial example of how increased choice may reduce freedom concerns the donation of blood. Following Titmuss (1970, pp.239–42), Singer has rejected the conventional market view expressed by Arrow (1972, p.350) that 'if to a voluntary blood donor system we add the possibility of selling blood, we have only expanded the individual's range of alternatives.' On the contrary, says Singer ([P.], 1978, p.213), by adding the option of selling blood we remove the option of voluntarily donating blood, in the sense that people are no longer free 'to give blood which cannot be bought, has no cash value'. Before the option of selling blood was introduced, people were free to give something that could not be purchased: after the option of selling blood was introduced, people are free only to give something that can also be purchased.

This argument has, however, been challenged on grounds that it does not show that a new option has *removed* an old option, but only that a new option has *devalued* an old option that remains available. When the selling of blood is allowed, what is lost is not the option of donating blood, but the option of donating it in circumstances in which other people are prevented from selling blood. What Singer is identifying, therefore, is not the *loss* of a freedom, but the *reduced worth* of a freedom. The net total of liberty has been increased (by the addition of a new option), though the net worth of liberty may have been reduced (if the value to blood sellers of the new option of selling is less than the value to blood donors of the old option of exclusive donoring). Moreover, as Lomasky (1983, p.257) says, if the Titmuss/ Singer argument were to be accepted, it would have wide-ranging consequences, since it could be used to justify extensive intolerance. On this argument, X could claim that a necessary condition of her freedom to do Q was that everyone else was prevented from doing P, because anyone doing P *vitiated* her freedom to do Q. If we accept the argument that since 'I shall not be able to place the same high value on my gift of blood if you are selling yours', therefore 'sale of blood is to be prohibited', we must also accept the conclusion that, for example, 'One's freedom to live in a God-fearing community is compromised by the presence of pagans'. This is a defence of illiberalism not liberalism – the tyranny of 'external' over 'personal' preferences, in [R.] Dworkin's terminology.

The fourth and final issue arising out of the notion of choices is whether, if a person freely chooses to relinquish freedom of choice, her resulting condition is one of freedom, because that condition was freely-chosen, or one of unfreedom, because it is a condition in which she can no longer freely choose to perform certain actions.

This is an issue which was raised when we were considering the absence of impediments conception of freedom; we concluded there that self-imposed impediments could reduce freedom if they prevented the agent from doing something with impunity. But viewing this issue exclusively in terms of the availability of choices conception, we may reach a different conclusion, because we must now take into account the fact that since self-imposition is itself a choice, there is a conflict between two kinds of choice; the initial choice which is performed, and subsequent choices which are thereby eliminated. (I will ignore the complicating possibility that by choosing to relinquish one kind of freedom, an agent may thereby widen her range of choice in relation to other kinds of freedom – a possibility that is frequently the outcome of entering into binding contracts (Schelling, 1984, pp.98–9).)

The question is, which kind of choice is sovereign? Writers who take the view that it is the subsequent choices which are crucial include Mill, who argues that self-enslavement is a condition of unfreedom;

'by selling himself for a slave, he abdicates his liberty; he foregoes any future use of it beyond that single act... He is no longer free... The principle of freedom cannot require that he should be free not to be free. It is not freedom, to be allowed to alienate his freedom.' (Mill, 1975, p.126)

For Dworkin ([G], 1975, p.180), similarly, preservation of future freedom justifies restrictions on contracts of self-enslavement. This view of Mill and Dworkin, endorsed by Benn and Weinstein (1971, p.211), has, however, been criticised by Harris ([CE], 1977, p.90), who points out that one could argue that 'the ultimate manifestation and assertion of one's own freedom is precisely the prerogative of terminating his freedom'. For example, the soldier who chooses virtual certain death for his country, thereby extinguishing his freedom along with his life, is performing the most extreme and genuine act of free choice. On this interpretation, the sovereign choice is the initial choice, since this is the act of commitment by which the agent chooses what kind of life she wants to lead, and affirms what kind of person she is.

However, it is important to note that what is being done here is to appeal to the conception of freedom as self-determination in order

to judge which of the choices – the initial or the subsequent choices –
is sovereign. The test of which choice represents the agent's sense of
what kind of a life she wants to lead or what kind of person she
wants to be is a test which incorporates the notion that freedom
consists in being a self-determined agent. Moreover, that test cuts
both ways, since, for example, the soldier's initial choice may not
represent his own real self, because he may have been unduly
influenced by social pressures when arriving at his decision. For a
similar reason, Fromm (1942) takes exception to the idea of
'freedom from freedom' (Fuller, 1955, p.1306). Exploring the
historical circumstances in which such a flight from freedom took
place on a mass scale in mid-20th century totalitarian states, Fromm
describes how secularism and democracy had destroyed people's
religious faith and respect for rulers, without providing them with
the capacity to use their new-found freedoms. As a result, says
Fromm, they chose to be released from the burden of freedom, and
to submit to totalitarian leaders such as Hitler, who claimed to be
'the greatest liberator of mankind', ordained by 'providence' to free
men from the demands of freedom and personal independence. But
in submitting to Hitler, says Fromm, the German people lost their
freedom, since their submission was not an authentic act of choice,
but an immature escape from reality. Whatever our opinion in such
cases, it is clear that the issue has switched from one of choice itself,
to one of the authenticity of the choice, and as such, the issues it
raises are best dealt with when we examine the self-determination
view of freedom.

So much for the four issues relating to the notion of choices – the
Z factor. The remaining issues raised by the availability of choices
conception of freedom relate to the notion of a chooser – the X
factor. Choice presupposes a chooser, but what constitutes a
'chooser'? Benn and Weinstein (1971, pp.209–10) argue that we
cannot describe as choosers people who are paranoid, compulsive,
neurotic, brainwashed, hypnotised or so entirely dominated by other
people that they cannot contemplate the possibility of disobeying
them. The reason for these various exclusions is that a 'chooser must
have a realistic understanding of the alternatives...a certain
minimum degree of rationality is necessary to freedom'. But is this
true? Is an irrational choice any less a choice than a rational choice?
An irrational choice may be a regrettable or unwise or damaging
choice, but does that mean it is not a choice? Many important

decisions are made every day by people who may not have 'a
realistic understanding of the alternatives'; for example, choices of
marriage partner, career, house, car, etc. Are these to be deemed the
decisions of unfree persons? It is true that people who act under
some kind of clinical compulsion do not appear to be self-controlled
in their decision-making, but the requirement of self-control is a
condition of freedom interpreted as self-mastery, not availability of
choices. However, in the case of brainwashing and hypnotism, Benn
and Weinstein are right to argue that free choice is absent – though
not because the actors are choosing irrationally, but because *they* are
not choosing at all, since other people are choosing for them.
Consideration of such cases is given later in this chapter, in the
discussion of freedom as self-determination.

One condition of choice that has been especially debated in the
literature on freedom is that of knowledge. A person who is ignorant
of some of the alternatives facing her, or who is unable to process
information about those alternatives, is often said to be unfree as a
chooser (Draughon, 1978, p.36; Cassinelli, 1966, pp.37–9).
Ignorance about oneself – lack of self-knowledge – is also deemed
by some writers to restrict one's capacity for free choice (Hampshire,
1965, p.92).

There are two separate questions involved in these claims about
the relation between freedom and lack of knowledge. The first
question relates to the restricted range of choices facing the ignorant
agent; the second question relates to the status of the ignorant agent
as a chooser. On the first question, it does not seem convincing to
say that ignorance of an option reduces one's freedom of choice with
respect to that option; it seems more convincing to say that such
ignorance reduces the chances that one will avail oneself of the
option, or that, as Day (1970, p.180) argues, such ignorance makes
one feel unfree to choose the option. Bryden (1975, p.64) asks,
rhetorically, of explorers – 'when men mistakenly thought the earth
to be flat, were they free to sail round the world?' – implying that
they were unfree to do so. But the ignorant explorers *were* free to sail
round the world and some did.

The situation is, of course, different if a person's ignorance is due
to her manipulation by other people. If I live in a totalitarian state
which controls information and feeds me false or selective facts, and
as a result I act in a way that is different from the way I would act if
I knew the truth, clearly I am less free as a result. But the reason why

the reason why I am less free is not because I am ignorant *simpliciter*, but because someone is preventing me from knowing the truth. Ignorance *in itself* is not a restriction on my freedom. Many (most?) of our choices are made in circumstances in which there is some degree of (uncoerced) ignorance on our part, if only because we cannot accurately predict the future. Are many (most?) of our choices to be regarded as to that extent unfree? The fact is that knowledge is one thing, and freedom interpreted as availability of choices is another. Increased knowledge may (or may not) lead to better choices, but not to increased choices.

The second question that arises out of the relation between freedom and lack of knowledge concerns the status of an ignorant person. This question raises deep issues about the connection between freedom and truth. Some religious writers claim that possession of spiritual truth is a prerequisite of free agency. 'And ye shall know the truth, and the truth shall make you free.' (St John's Gospel, VIII, 32). Similarly, rationalists such as Spinoza argue that reason liberates us from the servitude of error. In Berlin's words (1980, p.185), this is 'the notion that an increase of knowledge is *eo ipso* always an increase in freedom, i.e. an escape from being at the mercy of what is not understood'. However, the element of choice seems to have largely evaporated here. The agent is free if she has internalised the spiritual or rational order of the universe in her mind and in her conduct. But she does not appear to have to *choose* to internalise this spiritual or rational order. Moreover, when that order is internalised in her mind and conduct, she does not, in any normal sense, choose between alternative courses of action – the choice is made for her by the internalised system of spiritual or rational truth. Whatever notion of freedom is implied here, it is not a notion of freedom of choice; liberty is being interpreted as virtue or reason, and as such it falls within the category of freedom as self-mastery, discussed below.

Conclusion on the availability of choices conception of freedom

The conception of freedom as availability of choices is a politically popular and illuminating interpretation of freedom, focusing upon the sensible idea that an individual's freedom can be measured by the number of options open to her. However, considerable controversy surrounds the issues of what constitutes a genuine choice, and who is a genuine chooser. In the third conception of freedom, that of effective power, an attempt is made to deal with the first of these issues, by stipulating that a genuine choice is dependent upon the ability of the agent to exercise it. In the fifth conception of freedom, that of self-determination, an attempt is made to deal with the second of these issues, by stipulating that to be a genuine chooser, one must be autonomous. Nevertheless, there is considerable merit in the availability of choices conception of freedom. Most of the issues we have raised are less matters of intractable difficulty, than matters which require clarification if we are to make use of this conception. The central value of the availability of choices conception of freedom is that, just as the absence of impediments conception serves to elucidate one integral element of freedom – the nature of the Y factor – so the availability of choices conception serves to elucidate another integral element of freedom – the nature of the Z factor. In the conception of freedom as effective power, we will explore another attempt to elucidate both the Y and the Z factors.

3 Freedom as effective power

The conception of freedom in terms of effective power feeds off the contrast between nominal and real freedom. It focuses attention upon the issue of how freedom can become a reality rather than a formality – how freedom can be made meaningful to the agent. As such, it entails not the absence of impediments, but the ability to overcome impediments. 'In the fullest sense, freedom is not freedom *from* obstacles but freedom *over* them.' (Schneider, 1940, p.660). Freedom as effective power entails not only the availability of choices, but also conditions under which choices can actually be exercised (Sherover, 1984, p.485). Someone who is poor, or ill-educated, or sick, or disabled, or in any other way disadvantaged, lacks freedom on this conception. However, although the conception of freedom in terms of effective power thus appears to be distinct from the two previous conceptions, it has been argued that it is actually implicit within them. For instance, the Handlin (1961, pp.17–18) claim that implicit in the notion of absence of impediments is the assumption that an impediment cannot be overcome by the agent in question – i.e. that the agent lacks sufficient power to overcome the impediment. Similarly, it has been argued that the notion of effective power is implicit in the conception of freedom as availability of choice, in that the agent must be able to exercise the choice if the choice is to be properly described as a choice (Tawney, 1964, p.228).

Nevertheless, despite these links with other conceptions of freedom, the notion of effective power is a distinct conception, with an identity of its own. That identity is cast in terms of the practical meaningfulness of statements about freedom; it insists that for liberty to exist in any real sense, the agent must have the power to exercise it or the power to refrain from exercising it (Saunders, 1968, p.100; Bronfenbrenner, 1955, pp.161–2). If the availability of choices view of freedom is particularly popular in right-wing circles, the effective power view of freedom is particularly popular in left-wing circles. As the senior British Labour MP, Bryan Gould, put it ([B.], 1985, p.2), 'freedom is not, at bottom, an abstract, but rather a practical, thing. A freedom without the practical possibility of its being exercised is no freedom at all and has no meaning'.

The terms in which the notion of effective power is expressed vary from writer to writer. Some, like Dewey, use the term 'effective power' itself; others, such as the Fabians, express it in terms of ability to obtain commodities and services, or the possession of opportunity to develop skills and satisfy desires. Steiner (1974/5, p.48) writes in terms of material possession; '*freedom is the personal possession of physical objects*'. More important than these variations in the way it has been expressed, however, are different interpretations of effective power in relation to freedom. There are four interpretations of effective power that I want to consider. Only the first interpretation *identifies* freedom as effective power; in the other three interpretations effective power is understood as being *important* to freedom, without actually *being* freedom.

(a) Liberty means effective power

For some writers, liberty is synonymous with effective power: the possession of liberty presupposes the possession of effective power, and vice versa (Sherover, 1984, p.490). But many critics challenge this view, on the ground that freedom is conceptually quite distinct from power. Rehearsing this criticism, Partridge (1970, pp.94–5) claims that to run the two concepts together involves 'a distortion of ordinary language'; a poor person cannot afford to go to Monte

Carlo, but she is just as free to do so as is the rich person. Similarly, writes Parent (1974a, p.152), someone who suffers discrimination on grounds of race or wealth 'should express his moral outrage in the language of opportunity, not freedom'. In other words, we have perfectly appropriate words other than freedom to signify the idea of effective power, and it causes gratuitous confusion to employ the term 'freedom' when these other words can be used instead. Day (1977, pp.260–1) has pointed out that one cause of this confusion lies in the ambiguity of the word 'can', since the word 'can' may signify either freedom or ability. For instance, the statement 'I can fly to New York from London' may mean either that I am *free* to fly to New York from London (e.g. because my passport has not been impounded), or that I am *able* to fly to New York from London (e.g. because aircraft have been invented, they operate between these two cities, and I can afford the fare). But these two senses of the word 'can' are separate and must not be mixed up. Apart from conceptual confusions, failure to distinguish freedom from ability has important policy implications. As Miller (1983/4, p.70) points out, if we count every disability as a lack of freedom, then any attempt to maximise freedom in society would require a massive shift of resources towards the disabled.

It might, however, be replied that there is one situation in which it is legitimate to equate lack of effective power with unfreedom. This is the situation in which the lack of effective power in question is caused by human agency. If, for example, a poor person can attribute his lack of effective power to the fact that the economic system has been rigged against people like him, then his lack of effective power is equivalent to unfreedom. 'To say that someone is not free because not fed is to imply that someone wants him to starve' (Ryan, [A.], 1965, p.111). However, the unfreedom here lies not in the agent's lack of effective power in itself, but in the preventive action of other agents which has produced this lack of effective power. He is deprived by society of freedom by being subjected to a system of distribution that has been rigged against him. His poverty, i.e. his lack of effective power, is the result of his unfreedom, not its source.

(b) Liberty requires effective power

The second interpretation of the effective power view of freedom is that effective power is a necessary condition of liberty rather than synonymous with it (McCloskey, 1965, p.504). Although 'free' is not identical to 'can', 'free' does imply 'can'. The two notions are necessarily related, in that an increase in effective power entails more freedom, and a reduction in effective power entails less freedom.

However, this interpretation of the effective power view of freedom is vulnerable to the charge that it does not explain what freedom is, but only what its conditions are. A reply to this charge might take the form of arguing that the conditions of freedom are so integrally related to the concept of freedom that they cannot be separated from it. The meaning of freedom necessarily embraces its conditions, and if we ignore these conditions, we leave out of account a vital part of its essential meaning. Just as, say, the meaning of 'motor car' presupposes the notion of a road, since the idea of a motor car is unintelligible independently of somewhere to drive it, so, it may be argued, the meaning of freedom presupposes an account of its conditions. Freedom has a context, and that context includes the essential conditions under which it exists.

Even if we accept this reply, however, the question may be asked whether effective power *is* a necessary condition of freedom. It is true that in some circumstances physical power is a means to freedom, for example when someone pushes their way through a crowd of people. But in many other circumstances, physical power is irrelevant to freedom; for example, if I have the physical power or ability to drive a golf ball 300 yards down the fairway, my freedom is no greater than if I can only manage a 100 yard drive. What of economic power, which is the kind of power that advocates of the effective power view of freedom are most concerned with? On the effective power view, wealth or property necessarily confers freedom on its possessor, since it enables her to do things that she would be unable to do without such resources. Money opens doors and transforms nominal choices into real options: a rich person is thus freer than a poor person. However, it could be argued that money does not confer freedom on its possessor, but enables her to make greater use of her existing freedom (Machlup, 1969, p.126). Moreover, even if money can confer freedom on its possessor, it may not always do this. There are circumstances (admittedly rare) in which the possession of money closes doors rather than opens them. For example, access to working class organisations (and to the kingdom of heaven) may be made more difficult by a person's wealth.

(c) The worth of liberty requires effective power

The third interpretation of the effective power view of freedom is that effective power is essential if the agent's freedom is to be valuable or 'meaningful' to her (Parent, 1974a, p.163). Rawls (1972, p.204) states that while poverty and ignorance are not 'among the constraints definitive of liberty' they ought to be interpreted as 'affecting the worth of liberty', or the value to individuals of their freedoms. Weinstein (1965, p.151) adopts the same view in relation to illiteracy: if I am illiterate I am free to read, but that freedom is of little or no use or value to me.

However, this interpretation of effective freedom moves even further away from the task of explaining what freedom is. It describes not freedom, but the value of freedom. Moreover, it assumes a straightforward correlation between a person's effective power and the value of the liberty to which that power gives her access. But whether or not effective power makes a particular freedom meaningful and valuable is an entirely contingent matter. For example, no matter how easy the conditions for voting are made, some people decline to cast their vote in elections. This suggests that for them the suffrage is made no more valuable or meaningful by increasing their effective power to take advantage of it.

However, the latter part of this objection may be challenged on grounds that all it demonstrates is that if a person does not value a particular liberty in the first place, then increased access to that liberty will not be valued by her. Moreover, it overlooks the fact that the value of a freedom is not necessarily confined to the value placed upon it by the agent. If we make use of a 'third person' appraisal, we may say that an agent's increased power to avail herself of a liberty enhances the worth of that liberty to her, though she fails to acknowledge it. Nevertheless, the disjunction between freedom and the worth of freedom remains.

(d) The fair distribution of liberty requires effective power

The fourth interpretation of the effective power view of freedom is that effective power is a necessary condition for a fair distribution of liberty. This interpretation is, however, even more remote from the meaning of freedom itself. Indeed, it looks more like a definition of social justice than one of freedom (Parent, 1974a, p.162; Berlin, 1969, pp.125–6). McCloskey (1965, p.486) claims that 'probably all liberal and libertarian accounts of liberty confuse liberty with equal liberty or with fairly distributed liberty whereas liberty is one thing …and equality and justice other things'. Even if this is an exaggerated claim, the warning of Benn and Peters (1959, pp.212–13) is an apposite one – that the identity of freedom as a distinct moral ideal is devalued if we stretch it so far as to embrace other moral ideals.

Conclusion on the effective power conception of freedom

An implication that is often drawn from the identification of freedom with effective power is that freedom, like power, is a zero sum game – i.e. my freedom is necessarily at your expense and vice versa. We will examine this distributional implication in Chapter 5, where we will find additional reasons to those suggested here for caution in embracing the view that freedom is identical to power. It seems more convincing to argue that power is not so much a synonym for freedom, as a condition for its more effective utilisation, though we should bear in mind that this is an empirical assertion, not a conceptual truth. Nevertheless, the notion of effective power underlines the important distinction between nominal and real freedom, and draws attention to some of the social conditions for its meaningful exercise. In the next conception of freedom to be considered, freedom as 'status', we find the most concrete and contextual of all the conceptions of freedom. Here the social conditions necessary for freedom extend to a complete list of political and legal arrangements.

4 Freedom as status

Status is the fourth and last of the primarily *social* conceptions of freedom, and it is the most social conception of all, in that it identifies freedom as a position occupied by a person within a particular political and social structure. As such, freedom is something that is generally shared by members of a group – i.e. it is a collective as well as an individual attribute. The word 'status' implies that freedom is defined institutionally rather than behaviourally. Liberty is here conceived primarily as an ascription and only secondarily in terms of action; it is bound up more with who and what a person is than what a person does. Accordingly, a person may retain her full status of freedom, even when her physical movement is severely restricted. Gray (1980, p.512) gives a striking illustration of this, referring to the case of Socrates. 'Socrates could have claimed to have remained a free man throughout his imprisonment, since at no time did he exchange his status for that of a slave.' Nevertheless, the idea of action is never absent from this conception of freedom, in the sense that status confers the right to act in certain ways. Indeed, in some accounts of freedom as status, as we shall see, the activity of political participation is the central feature of the conception.

Historically, the status conception is the oldest conception of freedom. According to Mulgan (1984, p.8) and others, the original notion of liberty denoted the legal rights and privileges of the Greek citizen, including property ownership, freedom of movement and political participation. This was a status which marked off the 'free man' from the slave, alien, barbarian, woman and child (Feinberg, 1980, p.11). Many writers have noted the contrast between this original conception of freedom and subsequent conceptions, but they draw that contrast in different ways. Like Reed (1980, p.371), Crick (1967, pp.201–2) contrasts the 'earliest words we have for freedom', which are 'social status words', with the modern 'mechanical words' such as '"absence of constraint" or "unimpeded movement" of matter'. Arendt (1961b, p.148) contrasts the original 'condition of being free as a worldly tangible reality', with later notions of freedom 'as an attribute of thought or a quality of the will'.

There is also considerable controversy over the contemporary significance of the status conception of freedom. Berlin (1969, pp.155–7) takes a distinctly jaundiced view of it, describing it as a deeply felt aspiration 'to avoid ... being ignored or patronised, or despised, or being taken too much for granted', for which masses of people are willing to be bullied or misgoverned by their own kind rather than to be well treated by some alien ruler. Berlin (1969, p.160) also claims that it is 'an ideal which is perhaps more prominent than any other in the world today'. Crick argues, however, that such a jaundiced view is due to a basic misunderstanding of the status conception of freedom, confusing citizenship, which is what freedom as status entails, with nationalism, which freedom as status does not entail – indeed, nationalism poses a serious threat to citizenship. Crick (1967, p.211) concludes that it would be wrong to claim that freedom in the sense of status is a prominent ideal in the world today. While nationalism (Berlin's erroneous conception of status), may be prominent today, citizenship, the true conception of status, barely survived to the mid-19th century, after which it was crushed by nationalism itself, and by anti-statist liberalism.

Arendt, similarly lamenting the lapse of the civic ideal, traced its decline much further back in time, beginning with Epictetus, who, a slave himself, turned his face from the civic world from which he was excluded, and sought freedom in the inner world of the mind. Christians, not merely indifferent to the civic world, but hostile to it because it compromised spiritual values, found freedom in the soul's communion with God. For Arendt, then, the first steps away from the civic ideal were towards a mental conception of freedom. The next step (also identified by Crick) was towards a conception of freedom articulated by the classical liberals in terms of a private sphere of individual conduct to be protected from an interfering state (Arendt, 1961b, p.155). The final stage in the disparagement of the civic ideal came, says Arendt, with the rise of extreme nationalism in the form of twentieth century totalitarianism. Unlike Crick, however, Arendt (1961a, p.192) sees totalitarian nationalism not as swallowing up citizenship, but as further discrediting the activity of politics.

It is clear that Crick and Arendt want to rescue the conception of citizenship from what they see as its contemporary oblivion. For them the status of citizen is the essence of freedom; freedom is not an inner condition of thought, nor is it an outward condition of privacy – both of these are escapist notions adopted by people seeking to retreat from the real world. The proper sphere of freedom is the public, not the private, domain. This need not lead us down the slippery slope to nationalism and totalitarianism; indeed, citizenship is the best safeguard against such a slide, because in integrating people into their political and social order, it prevents the development of disillusionment which can produce a mass society and create conditions which are ripe for the emergence of nationalism and totalitarianism. In their analyses of the notion of status, Crick and Arendt have therefore shifted the emphasis away from the static conception of ascription, to the dynamic conception of action – in particular, political action. Indeed, for them both, freedom is virtually synonymous with politics (Crick, 1967, pp.205–7; Arendt, 1961a, pp.191,192,201).

There is one further element to be noted in the conception of freedom as status – the notion of the qualities displayed by the free person contrasted with the qualities displayed by the slave. 'A servile person is "alternately fawning and insolent"; a free man, having nothing to fear, is dignified and deliberate, and can look any man in the eye' (Feinberg, 1980, p.12). Crick refers to the qualities of 'disinterestedness and generosity – also a certain outgoing forcefulness', while Gibbs (1976 p.11) describes the character of the free person, in terms of decency; not capricious or arbitrary, but liberal-minded. This engaging picture of an upright, tolerant and courteous person constitutes one of the two intrapersonal dimensions of the status conception of freedom – the other being the feeling of integration and identification which it confers upon its recipient.

Clearly, the conception of freedom in terms of status is a rich and many-sided one. But it has not escaped criticism. One criticism is methodological – that the notion of status fails to satisfy the requirements of a valid conception of freedom laid down by MacCallum's triadic formula, in that it does not have either a Y factor (obstacle) or a Z factor (objective). That is to say, the status view of freedom simply asserts that X (an agent) is a free citizen; not free from Y (an obstacle) to do or be Z (an objective), but just a free citizen. Gray (1980, p.512) interprets this deficiency as a criticism of MacCallum's triadic formula, on the grounds that if MacCallum's formula cannot accommodate the status notion of freedom, then 'it is clearly defective'. But if we accept (as I do) the soundness of MacCallum's test, then if the notion of status fails to satisfy it, status cannot be a valid conception of liberty. However, the notion of status does satisfy MacCallum's test, since it contains implicitly within it both a Y factor and a Z factor; the citizen (X) is free from the restrictions (Y) which are imposed upon non-citizens, to perform all the actions (Z) that citizenship entails, and to develop the qualities characteristic of a citizen.

A more telling criticism is that the notion of status is not a conception of liberty, properly so-called, but a conception of identity, solidarity, community or fraternity. For Berlin (1969, p.158) 'it is something akin to, but not itself, freedom'; not the holding off of something or someone, which is what freedom is, but a desire to be integrated. Someone who is integrated into a community of like-minded people may well *feel* a sense of liberation, but in so far as this fact is relevant to freedom, it is a notion of *feeling free* rather than *being free*. However, there is no reason why we cannot acknowledge that there are both social and psychological elements in the status conception of freedom: status confers both interpersonal rights, and intrapersonal feelings, of freedom.

A third criticism attacks the view of status taken by Crick and Arendt for too closely identifying freedom with politics. Of course, to make the activity of politics possible, we need to have certain liberties, such as the freedoms of speech, publication, association and assembly. But this only means that politics requires liberties, not that politics and freedom are identical. By arguing that nothing outside the political sphere can be graced with the name of freedom, Crick and Arendt imply that the only free people are those engaging in politics, and that the freest people of all are the politicians, because they are engaged in politics most of the time. Crick and Arendt might reply to this criticism by arguing that unless we actively engage in politics, we are not in command of the circumstances of our own lives, since we are subject to the will of others. By idealising politics as the 'master science', following Aristotle, they are drawing attention to the important fact that self-government is the essence of freedom. But such an argument switches the issue to a different conception of liberty – that of self-determination – thereby diminishing the claim of the status conception to be an independent and distinct conception of freedom.

Conclusion on the status conception of freedom

In spite of the above criticisms, the status conception of freedom is noteworthy, not only because it is the original conception, but because of its collectivist claim that freedom may be a property of groups as well as of individuals. This collectivist dimension of freedom is often overlooked, but, as MacFarlane (1966, p.80) points out in criticising Berlin for his exclusively individualistic interpretation of liberty,

'My liberty, however, is rarely threatened because of what I am, *per se*; but because of what I am or stand for, as a member of a group. My liberty is threatened as a negro in Alabama, a Christian in East Germany or a trade unionist in Tanzania. It is as a member of one of these repressed groups that I suffer indignities and my area of personal freedom can be substantially increased only if these group restrictions are lifted.'

To interpret the freedom of a group as simply an aggregate of individual freedoms, is to ignore the fact that the clarion call of liberty is often invoked on behalf of oppressed groups rather than oppressed individuals. It is to defend their group identities, not their individual liberties, that many contemporary 'freedom fighters' have risked their lives.

The conception of freedom as status is the fourth and final conception which has an essentially social nature. There are two important psychological elements in the status conception – the sense of personal identity and recognition which membership of a group generates in the minds of those on whom the status is conferred, and the sense of liberal-mindedness which a person bearing the status of freedom displays. But these psychological elements are secondary to the institutional, legal and political rights and privileges which social status bestows. It is similar with the other social conceptions of freedom – there are some important psychological elements in each of them, but they remain primarily social conceptions.

By contrast, in the three conceptions that we are now to examine, primary emphasis is placed upon the psychological elements of freedom. The question such conceptions of freedom typically explore, is not 'in what circumstances is someone free?', but 'what is it like to be a free person?' In these conceptions, freedom is characterised more as a personal quality than a social condition. It must be noted, however, that this does not mean that there are no social elements in these intrapersonal conceptions of freedom; on the contrary, just as the interpersonal conceptions of freedom have important psychological dimensions, so the intrapersonal conceptions of freedom have important social dimensions.

This distinction between social and psychological conceptions of freedom, despite the fact that it is a somewhat blurred one, suggests a view which lies at the heart of my understanding of freedom – that the different conceptions of freedom are not necessarily mutually exclusive, but in many respects are complementary. Those writers who enunciate one of the four social conceptions of freedom draw our attention to one important aspect of freedom – namely, the notion of what it is for a person to be free *with respect to other people*; those writers who enunciate one of the three psychological conceptions of freedom draw our attention to another important aspect of freedom – namely the notion of what it is for a person to be free *in herself*. The point is that a person can have both social and psychological freedom simultaneously; she can be both free with respect to others, and free within herself. Moreover, more radically, I would argue that despite the significant distinctions that we have found between the four interpersonal conceptions themselves, and despite the significant differences that we shall see between the three intrapersonal conceptions themselves, it is conceivably possible for a person to enjoy freedom simultaneously in all seven senses. That is to say, there may be few impediments on what I can do, and I may have many options open to me, together with the capacity to exercise those options and the status of a citizen, and I may be largely self-determining in my conduct, doing what I want, and master of myself. In other words, although there are circumstances in which some of the seven conceptions of freedom may conflict with one another (for example, absence of impediments may lead to licence, the opposite of self-mastery) – circumstances in which their respective proponents will claim the palm for their favoured conception – there are circumstances in which the conceptions may be mutually compatible. This indicates that we can best understand these seven conceptions of freedom as each shedding some illumination upon different facets of a very complex concept. But this is to anticipate somewhat. Let us now turn to the first of the three essentially psychological conceptions of freedom – that of self-determination.

5   Freedom as self-determination

The conception of freedom as self-determination builds upon the notion of a free chooser to develop an explanation of what it is to be an independent agent. In doing so, however, it goes beyond the availability of choice conception of freedom, in that it demands that the agent has created her own pattern of existence in which she expresses her conception of the good, thereby affirming her sense of personal identity. 'The only freedom which deserves the name, is that of pursuing our own good in our own way' (Mill, 1975, p.18). The term 'authenticity' is sometimes used to signify this conception of freedom – indicating that freedom consists in performing actions that are 'fully our own', serving 'to express what we are like as persons . . . vehicles of self-disclosure' (Benson, 1987, p.481). The term 'autonomy' is also used to explain the notion of self-determination, since it encapsulates the idea of being subject to rules that we have personally endorsed ('auto' meaning 'self', and 'nomos' meaning 'rule'). As Rousseau puts it, 'obedience to a law which we prescribe to ourselves is liberty'. Self-determination presupposes the capacity for free will in the agent, since without that capacity, the agent cannot be said to make autonomous decisions.

In what follows, I examine three sets of arguments which seek to interpret freedom in terms of self-determination: (a) the extreme libertarian view that all human acts are self-determined and therefore free; (b) the modified or limited libertarian view that a small proportion of human acts are self-determined and therefore free; (c) the compatibilist view that self-determination, and therefore freedom, is coincidental with determinism.

(a) Extreme libertarianism

Asserting the doctrine of free will, extreme libertarians maintain that all human decisions and actions are initiated by the 'self'. This entails two propositions; first, that the agent is the sole cause of her actions; second, that in any given situation she could have acted otherwise than the way she did. Her personality and character are entirely determined by herself – she chooses even the pattern of her desires. '*A man may not only do what he pleases, but he may also please what he pleases*' (Davis, [W.H.], 1971, p.46). As a result, the agent is entirely responsible for the kind of person she is; she has created herself, warts and all (Berlin, 1980, p.178). She cannot claim that circumstances have made her what she is, for circumstances only exert as much power over her as she wills or allows them to exert. If she allows herself to be influenced by the mores of her society, then the responsibility is entirely hers, and if she drifts through life, following the path of least resistance, she is just as self-determining as if she imposes the most rigorous self-discipline upon herself; she cannot escape being free. Moreover, she can at any time change her character if she so wishes (Davis, [WH], 1971, p.35). This is the view adopted by existentialists such as Sartre, for whom people have no 'essence' imposed upon them either by nature or by environment; they are free to become whatever they choose, subject only to the constraints of physical laws. Chisholm (1966, p.23) puts this theory in terms of the notion of 'agent-causation': i.e. that when we act, we are, each one of us (like God?), a 'prime mover unmoved'. This is not to say that we always accomplish what we strive to bring about – on the contrary, we are often frustrated in our endeavours by circumstances that we have not chosen and cannot alter. But whenever we act, we do so freely in accordance with our chosen mode of interpreting our situation.

Extreme libertarianism has been much criticised. One criticism is that it may actually offer only a very restricted kind of self-determination, in that it may be satisfied with the notion that people accept responsibility for who they are and for the choices they make, but this is consistent with their having little or no say in the construction of the range of choices that face them. In itself, therefore, extreme libertarianism is a theory only of free-will, not freedom. If the extreme libertarian theorist demands more than cognitive self-determination, she must explain how agents have the capacity to fashion the world in which they live. But such an explanation shifts the discussion of liberty into the area of the effective power conception of freedom. Of course, in answer to this charge, the extreme libertarian could claim that free will is precisely all that freedom is; we may not hope to change our world, but we can change our response to our world, and therein lies our freedom. However, control over our responses seems to imply the conception of freedom as self-mastery rather than self-determination. Hence, the *wider* we stretch the notion of self-determination the closer we link it to the notion of effective power; and the *narrower* we confine the notion of self-determination, the closer we link it to the conception of self-mastery.

The second criticism is that extreme libertarianism depends upon an implausibly extensive interpretation of the notion of the 'self'. If the notion of the self is extended sufficiently in meaning, it can readily be interpreted as being the originating cause of virtually all of our actions. As Wilson (1958, p.68) points out, for example, 'If we include kleptomania as part of what we mean by "he", then the answer is that he did act freely, for it is nonsense to say that a man can be compelled by himself'. But such an all-inclusive interpretation of the self begs the central question of the conception of self-determination – namely the extent to which the self is itself determined. We will return to this critical issue in due course.

The third criticism is that extreme libertarianism seems to undermine the coherence of the notion of moral responsibility. At first sight, extreme libertarianism appears to offer a very thorough-going account of moral responsibility, in that total responsibility is attributed to the agent for everything she is, and therefore for everything she does. But as Lacey (1957/8, p.23) points out, if we 'momentarily recreate ourselves from scratch all the time, it is hard to see how we can blame a person for what he did in the past, because what is the connexion between that deed and his present state of mind?'

Connected to this criticism is the charge that the self-determination conception of freedom reduces human actions to random events. That is to say, if there is no causal process at work, freedom seems to be a matter of pure chance or accident. Frankfurt (1971, p.18) comments that 'whenever a person performs a free action, according to Chisholm, it's a miracle'. To claim that an agent causes her act, but that there are no prior causes which explain why she caused her act, seems to make free action a fortuitous and capricious event, without rhyme or reason (Fales, 1984, p.240). Of course, it could be argued that freedom just *is* arbitrary and purposeless action – a physical movement precipitated by the agent's uncaused will. But the conception of freedom as self-determination seems to demand something more determinate than random action. Alternatively, the extreme libertarian might reply to this charge of randomness by claiming that the agent exercises her free will under the guidance of her uncaused power of reason, and as a result attains order and coherence in her conduct. The difficulty with such a reply, however, lies in making sense of the notion of 'uncaused reason'. Since reasoning powers are developed within a social context, how can reason be immune to the forces of environmental determinism?

Fourthly, and most importantly, the extreme libertarian position has been criticised by extreme determinists for its gratuitous assumption that people can be self-determined. Extreme determinists argue that we are not the sole cause of our actions – we could not have acted otherwise than the way we did act. Skinner ([B.F.], 1973, pp.97,99) has developed the most thoroughgoing modern account of determinism. Freedom, says Skinner, is an illusion, invented by philosophers merely to flatter the human psyche by purporting to 'explain' in terms of autonomous action those areas of conduct that behavioural psychologists have not yet been able to explain in causal terms (Skinner, [B.F.], 1973, pp.97,99). Since there is no escape from causal control, what policy-makers must do is not to attempt the futile task of freeing people from all causal control, but to promote those forms of causal control that are most beneficial to human happiness. In particular, Skinner recommends 'non-aversive' controls, since these produce less human pain than do 'aversive' controls.

There are, however, serious flaws in Skinner's argument. For one thing, he appears to contradict himself in maintaining that there is no such thing as self-determination, yet that it is possible for us to choose one set of causal controls rather than another. If we are unavoidably programmed to behave in certain ways, then we are programmed to accept one set of controls rather than another, and if that programmed choice is for an aversive set of controls, then there is nothing Skinner or anyone else can do about it. Skinner's theory entails that an élite group of technologists knows the good, and knows which set of causal controls will achieve it. But if everything is determined, then the élite's conception of the good and the means to achieve it, is itself determined. Indeed, Skinner's own ideas are determined, as is his would-be influence in recommending non-aversive controls. Hence, whether or not Skinner's vision of a society governed solely by non-aversive controls is ever put into practice, is an issue that is already decided.

Skinner's theory can also be challenged for its lack of empirical verification. He claims that assertions of autonomy are due to contemporary ignorance of some of the causes which determine human behaviour. But why should he assume that further research will reveal these undiscovered causes? It is equally plausible to conclude from our present ignorance of some of the causes of human behaviour that there are no such causes, and that some human conduct is the result of genuinely autonomous choice. When Skinner criticises libertarians for cherishing the unproven belief that people have free will, is he himself not open to the converse charge that he is cherishing the unproven belief that people do not have free will? Until the empirical evidence is produced, neither side can claim victory. Moreover, many of the deterministic controls identified by Skinner are not *causes*, properly so-called, of human behaviour, but simply reasons or explanations for human actions. We may be able to explain why someone performed an action without presupposing that the action was determined. For example, we may say that the reason why a person chose to invest money in gold, was because she was much influenced by an economic forecast; but that does not mean that her choice was *determined* by the forecast. 'Freedom does not require that no one else influence one's environment.' (Scribner, 1972/3, p.25).

The extreme determinist case, that all our actions are determined, is therefore flawed. But the extreme libertarian case, that all our actions are free, is also flawed. The truth may lie somewhere in between these two positions, in a compromise view that, while many of our actions are determined, some of our actions are free. This is the view of 'limited libertarianism'. Alternatively, the truth may lie in some form of synthesis between libertarianism and determinism, whereby a person may be said to be free even though her actions are determined. This is the view known as 'compatibilism'. I will consider these two views in turn.

(b) Limited libertarianism

Limited libertarianism concedes that much human conduct is caused by circumstances beyond the agent's control, but it maintains that some human conduct is freely chosen by the agent: 'self-determination provides a basis for saying (sometimes) "the buck stops here"' (Ferré, 1973, p.169). Campbell, who is a leading proponent of limited libertarianism, delineates the part of human conduct that is determined by circumstances beyond the agent's control as the sphere of non-moral choice. This sphere of human conduct is the part which is 'in character' – i.e. comprising actions that arise out of a person's settled personality and disposition – and is manifested in a given pattern of desires. Since a person's character is formed (determined) by heredity and environmental experiences, choices that an agent makes which are 'in character' cannot be 'categorically' free, because they simply give effect to the strongest desire in his nature. He has no capacity to determine the structure of his desires, and he cannot but act on his strongest desire (Campbell, 1962, p.339). Such a choice may be an *act* of will , but it is not an *effort* of will, and so it is not an act of free will, since the will is simply an expression of his character, and if we possessed perfect knowledge of that character we could predict with certainty what his non-moral decisions would be.

The part of human conduct which, according to Campbell, is not determined by circumstances beyond the agent's control is the sphere of moral choice. This sphere of human conduct is the part which is 'out of character', comprising actions that arise out of a person's decision to place her duty above her strongest desire. We are 'categorically' free when, and only when, we face up to our moral duty; in every other choice that we make we merely give effect to our predetermined order of desires, but here we suspend that order, and in doing so we perform an *effort of will*, not just an *act of will* (Campbell, 1966, pp.346–7). An act of free will, i.e. an act which involves an effort of will, cannot be predicted with certainty, since even if we possess perfect knowledge of a person's character, we can never know whether she will act 'out of character' (Chisholm, 1966, p.25).

Several criticisms have been made of Campbell's attempt to show that our moral choices are acts of self-determination and therefore free. One criticism is that even if his argument is accepted, it does not show that human beings possess very much freedom. Campbell (1970, p.105) admits that since very few of our choices *are* moral choices, then 'Over by far the greater area of human choices... the free will we are defending has no business. There is just nothing for it to do'. The reason why Campbell restricts self-determination, and therefore freedom, to the narrow area of moral choice is that he assumes that people who act on their strongest desire cannot be free because they are merely acting 'in character'. The question that Campbell has to answer, however, is 'why shouldn't we describe actions that are 'in character' as free?' As Dilman (1961/2, p.46) argues, 'Is not an action which flows from the agent's own nature a free action *par excellence*?'

Campbell's answer to this question is of course to assert that a person's character is not within her power to determine – an assertion that will be examined in a moment. But if so, how can Campbell deal with the claim that someone who acts in accordance with her moral duty is responding to her strongest desire, and therefore is acting 'in character'? (Anderson, 1981, p.40). On this view, all our acts are due to our desires, and therefore all our acts are determined by our pre-formed character, and so there can be no freedom at all in Campbell's sense of self-determination. A similar conclusion may be reached even if we interpret the moral duty not as a desire, but in the way in which Campbell himself interprets it – as an ethical imperative independent of desire – since ethical imperatives may be seen to be just as much a part of the agent's character as are her desires. On this view, the conflict is between two different aspects of the agent's character, duty and desire, and even if duty prevails, there is no freedom involved. Indeed, taking a moral stand may be the most vivid expression of a person's character.

This criticism is bound up with a wider attack on Campbell's separation of a person's 'self' from her 'character'. Surely one's self *is* one's character, and one's character *is* one's self? To act 'out of character' is not, in ordinary parlance, a literal but a metaphorical expression, used to signify that someone has acted in an unexpected way, not to suggest that she has suspended all her character-determined predispositions. Campbell's idea that the agent's 'self' somehow stands outside her 'character', capable of acting independently of it, seems bizarre. If the moral decision is not part of the agent's character, it is not *her* act at all, so the criticism runs, for how can anyone act out of character and yet still *be* that character?

Campbell's notion of a self which is independent of character is also vulnerable to the charge that this independence cannot be watertight, since the decisions of a person's self must modify her character. For example, repeated choices by the self of morally virtuous actions will so modify the agent's character that moral virtue will become more and more habitual, and therefore begin to form part of the agent's character. Hence, as Anderson (1981, p.401) observes, 'in asserting one's free will in the *present*, one will likely be limiting one's freedom in the *future*'. On fewer and fewer occasions will the agent's acts of moral virtue be free acts, since the self will be acting more and more 'in character' rather than 'out of character'. Paradoxically, then, the more we perform the only acts that constitute freedom, the more our freedom is reduced. 'The more inclined we are generally to do our duty, the less free we are. Naturally good people will seldom, if ever, be free.'

(c) Compatibilism

The compromise position adopted by limited libertarians such as Campbell, to the effect that some of our actions are determined while others are free, is not, therefore, an entirely satisfactory mode of reconciliation between libertarianism and determinism. An alternative mode of reconciliation is that offered by compatibilists. Compatibilists see no conflict between libertarianism and determinism; indeed they argue for a synthesis between them, claiming that a person's actions may be simultaneously free and determined.

One form of compatibilism is the oft-expressed view that a person's actions may be free in the sense of being uncoerced, but determined in the sense of being caused (Aune, 1962, p.397). That is to say, provided X is not prevented by Y from doing Z, she is free to do Z, despite the fact that her decision to do Z may be entirely caused by her formed character (Foot, 1966, p.95). Hobbes and Hume both enunciate this view, as does Ayer (1946, p.43) who argues that causation does not compel actions, it simply explains them. A variant of this form of compatibilism is the view that a person may be free to choose to do what she wants, but her wants are determined; she can choose to do what she wants, but she cannot choose to want what she wants. She is bound – determined – to do what she wants if she can; when she can do what she wants, she is free (Kenny, 1973, p.91). Even though all her choices are determined, she is free when her desires are satisfied, and unfree when her wishes are frustrated (Zimmerman, [M.], 1965/6, pp.417,419).

However, this form of compatibilism is unsatisfactory, since it depends on the employment of conceptions of freedom other than that of self-determination. What it boils down to is the assertion that a person may be free in the sense of 'absence of impediments' or 'availability of choice' or 'effective power' or 'doing what one wants', while being unfree in the sense of self-determination. This assertion is indisputable, but it is a reconciliation not of freedom defined as self-determination with determinism, but of freedom defined as absence of impediments or as availability of choices or as effective power or as doing what one wants, with determinism. Indeed, it is a denial of self-determination (Gallagher, 1964, p.481).

A rarer form of compatibilism is the view that our freedom lies in the very recognition, acceptance and affirmation of the fact that we are determined. There are a number of versions of this form of compatibilism, one of which is constructed in terms of people coming to terms with their socialised desires. Although a man's desires are the result of social conditioning, he can make them his own, so to speak, by 'identifying with them in his reflective judgings' (Young, 1980b, p.573; cf Bergmann, 1977, p.238). Accepting, not resisting, the kind of person we are by nature and nurture is often a source of liberation, as many homosexuals have found. Another version of this form of compatibilism is offered by Rousseau, Kant, Hegel and Marx, to the effect that we are free only when we embrace the laws that govern human life and spirit. Here freedom exists not in the absence of necessity, but in the agent's understanding of that necessity by which she is governed: indeed it is only when her self-directed activity coincides with the objective requirements of existence that she is free.

However, this form of compatibilism is unsatisfactory. Coming to terms with either internal or external necessity seems to confirm one's helplessness, rather than to exemplify one's freedom. 'I do not become free by becoming conscious that I am not' (Ayer, 1946, p.40). Since, as Bernstein (1983, p.123) points out, the very act of recognition of necessity must itself be determined, this form of compatibilism is simply disguised determinism.

A third form of compatibilism is the assertion that while a person's actions are determined, in the sense that they are always attributable to her character, that character has been formed by the agent herself in making decisions over a number of years. Hence her actions are determined, but they are determined by her self-determined character. However, this form of compatibilism is less a reconciliation of libertarianism and determinism than a disguised form of extreme libertarianism, since the person herself is held ultimately to be entirely responsible for all the choices she makes. A modified version of this view which escapes such a charge is that while all our actions are determined, we ourselves contribute to the processes which determine them. The circumstances which form our character include our desire to mould it in our own particular way (Mill, 1879, p.426). This very persuasive view suffers, however, from the difficulty of establishing an independent source for the self-determining elements in the determination process. It could be argued that the agent's desire to mould her character in a particular way is itself the result of conditioning, and that therefore this version of compatibilism is a disguised form of determinism.

Conclusion on the self-determination conception of freedom

Despite the difficulties inherent in extreme and limited libertarianism and in compatibilism, they do capture an important dimension of freedom – that of people being the authors of their own actions. The idea that at least in some respects people can freely will to do this or that action, or to be this or that kind of person, is an enduring intuition, and an important part of our perception of the nature of freedom. However, these forms of self-determination concentrate on the task of showing how people can resist (or come to terms with) external determination in shaping their own character for themselves, and they leave to one side the problem of how people can shape their world – a problem addressed by the effective power conception of freedom (as we have seen). Moreover, they lack a thoroughgoing account of human wants. That is to say, they suggest that a person's freedom consists in her doing what she herself *really wants* to do; but they do not examine the conceptual implications of such a suggestion. In the remaining two conceptions of freedom to be considered – doing what one wants, and self-mastery – these implications are explored.

6 Freedom as doing what one wants

The appeal of the conception of freedom in terms of 'doing what one wants' is obvious, in that, as Neely (1974, pp.36–7) says, 'Freedom does, after all, seem to have something to do with doing as you please'. Indeed, it may be considered to be a more fundamental conception of freedom than its five predecessors, in that it seems to be presupposed by all of them. For instance, 'absence of impediments' may be interpreted as absence of restrictions on an agent preventing her from doing what she wants to do. Poole (1975, p.12) argues that the very nature of what constitutes an impediment to a person's freedom depends on that person's wants; something will serve as an impediment to my freedom if I have a desire that it frustrates, but will not serve as an impediment to my freedom if it frustrates none of my desires – indeed, it might even serve as a means to my freedom if it facilitates the satisfaction of my desires.

> 'A wall, for example, will be in my way if I want to reach the other side; it may be a prerequisite of my activity, if I want to paint a mural. Whether I conceive of that wall as an impediment or not, will depend on what I conceive my wants, or my potential wants, to be.'

Similarly, 'availability of choices' may be taken to refer to options that allow me to choose to do what I want to do; 'effective power' may be taken to mean the capacity to satisfy my desires; 'status' suggests a position of privileged access to social goods desired by everyone; and 'self-determination' may be interpreted as directing my life as it pleases me to do.

However, these links between the conception of freedom as doing what one wants and the five previous conceptions should not be exaggerated. As we have seen in earlier discussions, many writers insist that impediments, choices, power, status and free will are not necessarily connected to the agent's desires. If I am prevented from doing something by an impediment, I am unfree to do that thing, whatever my wants happen to be. In Poole's example, the artist who needs the wall to paint her mural is nevertheless prevented by the wall from getting to the other side, whether she wants to or not. Similarly, a choice is a choice whether I welcome it or not; my power to do something is independent of whether I want to do it; status may or may not be valued by me; and my free will may actually be manifest only in acting contrary to my desires. At any rate, it seems clear that these five conceptions are not dependent for their credibility upon the conception of freedom as doing what one wants.

Ten objections have been made to the wants conception of freedom. The first is that it is an entirely unrealistic conception of freedom: 'what shall we make of the phrase "a man can do what he wants"? In no society ever, could a man "do what he wanted", in any area' (Berki, 1968, p.367). We are limited in doing what we want to do by the forces of both nature and society. For example, any desire that I may cherish to be the most famous person in the world is doomed to frustration. This objection does not, however, *invalidate* the 'doing what one wants' conception; it simply indicates that in this view of liberty complete or total freedom may never be possible, and so we must adjust the conception to read 'freedom lies in doing those things that one wants to do that are within the bounds of practicability'. This adjustment is in line with similar qualifications imposed on the five previous characterisations, for none of them can postulate complete or total freedom; we are ineluctably impeded by gravity; we have no choice of flying to Mars; no one can be all-powerful; status never confers absolute privilege; and I cannot determine my genetic structure. However, the question of which wants are judged to be within the realm of practicability is not always easily answered.

The second criticism of the wants conception of freedom arises from the opposite perspective from that adopted by Berki. There is a sense in which we might be said to act always on our desires, in that everything that we do is prompted by some desire or other. Many writers enunciate this view of human conduct, including Plamenatz (1968, p.110). If this is true, and we always do what we want to do, then on the wants conception of freedom, we are always free. But, as Dworkin points out, this is an unacceptable conclusion, since it destroys the basis of any distinction between freedom and constraint. If I always do what I want to do, then even when I act under constraint I am free. For example, since I want to save my life, I give up my money to the highwayman, and I am thus doing what I want. On this view, coercion does not make me unfree, but merely subjects me to a new situation in which, as usual, my strongest desire, whatever it now is, will prevail. Coercion may well alter the desires that I have, or the priority in which I put those desires, but it cannot prevent me acting upon my desires. 'Just as one cannot force open a door that swings freely on its hinges one cannot force a man whose will swings willingly in any direction' (Dworkin, [G.], 1970b, pp.368,383). However, the assumption upon which this hypothesis rests is false; we do not always do what we want, though we may always do what we intend. When I am coerced, I may intend to submit to the coercion, but I do not want to, and so on the wants conception of freedom, I am not free (Dworkin, [G.], 1970b, pp.371,375–6; Frankfurt, 1975, pp.113–4; Thalberg, 1983, p.103); Zimmerman, [D.], 1981a, p.128).

The third criticism is that the wants conception of freedom entails that questions of freedom are only raised in connection with people's desires. Hence, where there are no desires or wants, no question of freedom can arise, and so in any area of conduct where I have no desires at all, I cannot be made unfree. This implies that if restrictions are imposed upon me which do not conflict with any desire of mine, they are not properly called restrictions, since they do not reduce my freedom – they do not prevent me from doing what I want to do. Many writers, including Dryer, Mabbott, Scott, Plamenatz and Smith, readily accept this implication. For instance, Dryer (1964, p.445) claims, when referring to a prisoner who has no desire to leave his cell, that 'His freedom can no more be said to be impaired than is that of someone who would not choose to throw himself off a cliff and is protected by a high fence from going over the edge'.

However, many critics object to this view, because it reduces freedom to a purely mental condition. Steiner (1974/5, p.34), for example, argues that being locked in a prison cell makes a prisoner unfree to go to the theatre, whether or not he desires to do so. Feinberg (1980, pp.39 40) insists that we must not confuse freedom with contentment; freedom involves action, but contentment does not. Suppose someone can plug himself in to a 'contentment machine', says Esheté (1982, p.498), 'it would be strange to regard this contented man who does not bring about anything as free... although contentment is possible in complete passivity, freedom, though not always reducible to freedom of action, is essentially connected to activity'.

In one sense, these critics are right; freedom is not *synonymous* with contentment. A slave may be perfectly contented, in that she has no desire to do things incompatible with her slavery, but she is nevertheless a slave and, as such, unfree in an interpersonal sense of freedom. If she subsequently becomes discontented, she is no less free than before in an interpersonal sense, even though her attitude to her condition has undergone fundamental change.

However, in another sense these critics are mistaken, since, as Smith (1977, p.236) observes, 'Contentment, or satisfaction, is a *kind* of freedom'. Want satisfaction may not be *all* that there is to freedom, but it is 'one of the many senses of the term'. The contented slave is clearly unfree in an interpersonal sense of freedom, but may very well be free in an intrapersonal sense of freedom – free from frustration. Freedom may not be a *purely* mental phenomenon, but that is not to say it cannot have *any* mental manifestations. This observation repeats the point made frequently in this book – that freedom has both an interpersonal and an intrapersonal dimension. More controversially, Smith argues that the contented slave may be free even in the interpersonal sense – if, after being released, she chooses to return to slavery. This may be true, though only by shifting the discussion to the availability of choices conception of freedom (the second of the four interpersonal conceptions): the slave is not free interpersonally because she is content, but because she has chosen slavery. Smith's claim also faces the difficulty (that we rehearsed when examining the availability of choices conception) of deciding which choice is sovereign – the choice of slavery, or the subsequent limitation of choice entailed by slavery.

An advocate of the 'doing what one wants' view of freedom might, alternatively, reply to the third criticism by arguing that freedom implies a desire, if not necessarily of every person who possesses it, at least of some person who possesses or has possessed or might possess it. Bryden (1975, p.63) argues that a restriction on, or a guarantee of, a freedom necessarily presupposes that *someone* must have wanted, or might want in the future, to do the thing restricted. For example, while it is true that the fact that British citizens are free to vote does not entail that any of them wants to vote, it does entail that 'some British citizens at some time wanted, were presumed to want, or might come to want to vote'. However, while Bryden may be right to say that there is no point in introducing laws designed to remove or confer freedoms unless someone's wants are involved, this does not establish any conceptual link between freedom and desire. Moreover, whatever link does exist, it is a very weak link, since it is a link not between my freedom and my desires, but between *my* freedom and *someone else's desires or possible desires*.

Bryden might reply to this point by arguing that any account of a person's desires must include the desires or possible desires of everyone else, on the ground that she herself might adopt any such desire in the future. On this view, as Scott (1956, p.185) puts it, liberty 'is freedom to do whatever we *may* want to do in that field, and, as there is no knowing what we *may* want to do, it is freedom to do everything in that field whether or not we *will* want to do it'. But suppose I *never* want to do the act restricted; in what sense have I been unfree to do it if freedom is defined as doing what one wants? In Bryden's argument the link between freedom and desire has been diluted to the point where he is in danger of shifting from the wants conception of freedom to the availability of choices conception of freedom, for it is on that view of freedom that the notion of keeping one's possible options open for the future is really appropriate, and the issue of whether those options are, or ever will be, desired by the agent, is strictly irrelevant. Bryden is entitled to reply, however, that, as Cohen puts it, 'I may resent my lack of freedom to do what I have no wish to do: Soviet citizens who dislike restrictions on foreign travel need not want to go abroad.' (Cohen, [G.A.], 1983, p.18).

The third criticism – that the 'doing what one wants' view of freedom confuses freedom with contentment – is paralleled by a fourth criticism that it confuses 'being free' with 'feeling free'. Although there is no necessary connection between 'doing what one wants' and 'feeling free' – Day (1970, p.180) is mistaken in claiming that the latter presupposes the former – nevertheless, doing what one wants may produce a feeling of contentment which in turn may make the agent feel free even when she is actually unfree. In so far as there *is* this connection between want-satisfaction and feeling free, the wants conception of freedom is vulnerable to the charge of confusing being free with feeling free (Flathman, 1987, p.30). However, in reply to this charge, it could be claimed that the whole point of having freedom is to feel free, and that it would be just as much a mockery to attribute freedom to someone whose freedoms do not make her feel free, as it would be to attribute freedom to someone whose poverty prevents her from making effective use of her freedom. 'Ultimately we care about being free because there are occasions on which we want to feel free' (Dworkin, [G.], 1970b, p.380). But the critics argue that the question of whether being free makes one feel free is a question that relates to the value of freedom not to its meaning, just as the question of whether one can make effective use of one's freedom is a question that relates to the worth, not the existence, of freedom. In any case, it is not true that the whole point of having liberty is to feel free: the possession of freedom may serve many other purposes, including the promotion of scientific and technical progress.

Perhaps the proper significance of the notion of feeling free is not that it uniquely captures the essence of being free, but that it is an alternative notion of freedom to that of being free. It could be argued that each of these two notions, feeling free and being free, is an independently valid dimension of freedom, offering its own insight into the nature of freedom, and little is gained by asserting that either one or the other is the true or authentic or basic notion. Dworkin ([G.], 1970b, pp.379–81) defends the notion of feeling free, not by arguing that feeling free *means* being free, since he acknowledges that the slave who 'accepts the fetters that bind him' is unfree because 'fetters are fetters, even if they are accepted fetters', but by maintaining that feeling free is another sense of freedom, expressing the truth that in willingly obeying his master, the slave acts freely. However, the attempt to separate the notion of 'feeling free' from the notion of 'being free' runs up against the criticism that if I *feel* free, I feel that I *am* free. Hence feeling free implies a conception of freedom (being free) over and above the mere feeling itself. If there were not a state of *being* free, there would not be something that I could *feel* myself to be. Nevertheless, the idea of feeling free does seem to be an enduring element in our conception of freedom, albeit one that is parasitic upon the idea of being free.

The fifth criticism of the 'doing what one wants' conception of freedom concerns the notion of 'wants'. If the wants that a person has are entirely conditioned by her environment, then acting upon those wants seems to exemplify unfreedom rather than freedom; at any rate, she would be unfree in the sense of not being self-determined. If, however, her wants were genuinely autonomous, then she would be free in both the wants and the self-determination senses of freedom – in doing what she wants, she would be doing what *she* wants (Arneson, 1985, p.432). The difficulty is, of course, to distinguish which of a person's wants are autonomous – an issue we explored in the discussion of the self-determination conception of freedom. Furthermore, if the 'wants' that a person has are due to some ignorance or misunderstanding on the agent's part, and would change if that ignorance or misunderstanding were corrected, then it is arguable that if she acts upon her misguided wants she is unfree rather than free (Zimmerman, [D.], 1981b, p.364). These two considerations indicate the complexity of the notion of wants. We cannot assume that we always know what people's own wants are, and therefore we cannot assume that when they act ostensibly upon their wants, they are free.

The sixth criticism of the 'doing what one wants' view of freedom is that it gives rise to the paradox that a person may be simultaneously free and unfree. Take, for example, the unhappy kleptomaniac who on one level wants to steal, but on another level wants not to want to steal. On the wants conception of freedom, therefore, whether she steals or not, she is both free and unfree. Of course, this paradox is not confined to kleptomaniacs; wherever a person's wants come into conflict with one another, the same difficulty arises of simultaneous want-satisfaction and want-frustration.

Several attempts have been made to resolve this paradox by seeking to identify which of the wants is more closely related to the agent's freedom. For example, we might distinguish between 'internal' and 'external' wants; internal wants being natural and spontaneous, external wants being artificial and imposed from outside the agent. Only if a person acts on her internal wants is she free, since if she acts on her external wants she is not acting 'authentically' (Dilman, 1961/2, p.49). Or we may follow Neely (1974, p.45) in distinguishing between 'low priority' desires and 'high priority' desires, to conclude that the more a person acts on the latter, the freer she is, because 'The desires that are ranked high are those more intimately identified with the self' (Esheté, 1982, p.499). Dworkin makes use of a similar distinction couched in terms of the notion of identification: only if the agent identifies with her reason for doing some act, does she act freely (Dworkin, [G.], 1970b, p.382).

A number of other writers distinguish between first-order and second-order desires; first-order desires are immediate desires, second-order desires are desires about desires. If I act on my first-order desires I am not free unless I also desire to act on these first-order desires. Hence the kleptomaniac, who has a first-order desire to steal, will only be free in stealing if she wants to want to steal – i.e. if her second-order desire endorses her first-order desire. She will be unfree in stealing if she wants not to want to steal, i.e. if her second-order desire is in conflict with her first-order desire (Frankfurt, 1975, p.114; 1971, pp.8ff). The reason why the endorsement of second-order desires is necessary to freedom is that, where they prevail, the agent is exercising the capacity to evaluate wants, not just to satisfy them.

However, these suggested solutions to the paradox of simultaneous satisfaction and frustration of wants raise various difficulties. One difficulty is to decide which desire comes into which category. For example, which of the kleptomaniac's desires is the internal desire? (Is the urge to steal more, or less, internal to her than the desire not to have that urge?) With which desire does she most identify? (Does she see herself as someone who is not a kleptomaniac?) Another difficulty is that of the problem of an infinite regress (Zimmerman, [D.], 1981b, p.358). For example, a person may have a first-order desire to smoke, and a second-order desire not to want to smoke. But only if that second-order desire is endorsed by a third-order desire – e.g. to be the kind of person who does not want to smoke – would action on the second-order desire be deemed to be free on the wants conception of freedom, since only if the agent *wants* to have the second order desire, is smoking something that she really wants to give up. But the third-order desire in turn must be endorsed by a fourth-order desire if it is to be the guarantor of freedom – the agent must want to have her third-order desire if action in accordance with it is to be deemed free. And so on; each order of desire demands a further order, and there is, therefore, an infinite regress. We might try to avoid this infinite regress by simply stipulating that the second-order desire is more authentic than the first-order desire. But on what basis can such a stipulation be founded? What is more authentic about second-order desires? What is to prevent a second-order desire being less authentic than a first-order desire? (Watson, 1982, p.108). As Thalberg (1983, pp.111–2) puts it, 'why should we assume that our "life plans" and "systems of ends"... are more representative of us than our most savage, incoherent whims?' Surely a person can equally well identify with her first-order wants? (Young, 1980a, p.37).

In any case, the above suggested solutions are in danger of moving beyond the 'doing as one wants' view of liberty in an attempt to apply it. By stipulating that some desires are more closely related than others to the agent's authentic or real self, these solutions are interpreting the wants conception of freedom as 'doing what one *really* wants'. This interpretation shifts the focus of attention away from the notion of wants to the notion of authenticity, and in so doing raises the question of whether the wants conception has been abandoned for either the self-determination or the self- mastery conception of freedom. A person may affirm herself by doing something that she does *not* want to do (Dworkin, [G.], 1970b, p.377).

The seventh criticism of the wants conception of freedom is that it implies the counter-intuitive idea that one way of increasing my freedom is to restrict my desires. 'If freedom were doing as one pleases, it would not take much of a twist to equate it with pleasing as one does' (Neely, 1974, p.38). According to Rousseau (1963, p.48), 'That man is truly free who desires what he is able to perform, and does what he desires'. If my freedom consists in doing what I want, then I can increase that freedom either by improving my ability to satisfy my wants, or by tailoring my wants to suit my ability. The latter strategy may well be the more successful, since it depends on the agent alone and it affords a guaranteed way of maximising freedom; by giving up all desires which I cannot satisfy, I will become completely free. Epictetus maintained that 'freedom is not acquired by satisfying yourself with what you desire, but by destroying your desire'. But surely, the critics argue, it is counter-intuitive to maintain that I can increase my freedom by reducing my desires (Benn, 1988, p.132). As Fain (1958, p.372) wryly remarks, 'there would seem to be two methods of freeing the prisoner. One would be to remove the chains; the other would be to present the prisoner with a copy of Epictetus'. Behind this satirical comment lies the heart of the matter – that the 'two methods of freeing the prisoner' actually reflect two different senses of freedom; an interpersonal sense (requiring the removal of the chains), and an intrapersonal sense (requiring the prisoner to give up her desire to leave the cell). Hence, when Steiner (1974/5, p.34) argues that 'ridding oneself of the desire to do an action which is prevented by another, does not render one free to do that action', he is right only in indicating that an agent who gives up a desire does not thereby become *interpersonally* free, but he is wrong to imply that such an agent cannot thereby become *intrapersonally* free.

This brings us to the eighth criticism of the wants conception of freedom, that it gives rise to the celebrated paradox that we may be 'forced to be free' if our desires are curtailed by some external agent. Rousseau was the originator of this paradox, arguing that the enforcement of our 'general' or real will over our 'particular' or immediate will is the condition of our freedom. 'Whoever refuses to obey the general will shall be compelled to do so by the whole body. This means nothing less than that he will be forced to be free' (Rousseau 1973, p.177). Sterba and Kourany (1980/1, p.518) claim that if a person's unruly desires are coercively overcome in order to promote her higher-order life plans, then on the wants conception of liberty, her freedom is not impaired but secured. This 'implies that we can make prisoners and slaves free men by conditioning them not to want anything else' (Parent, 1974a, p.159). But making people unable to desire something seems an odd way of increasing their freedom (Arneson, 1985, p.428). As Day (1970, p.191) somewhat brutally retorts, 'One might as well argue that ... the way to dispose of the problem of a prisoner's unfreedom of movement is to amputate his limbs'. These critics have a point, though it should be noted that Rousseau is not arguing that freedom entails the suppression of desires *per se*, but only the suppression of desires that conflict with the general will.

The ninth criticism of the wants conception of freedom is that there is an element of circularity in it. It defines freedom in terms of wants, but often our wants are themselves largely fashioned by our freedom, in that many of our desires are shaped 'adaptively' by what we are free to do. Other desires are shaped 'counter-adaptively', i.e. as a reaction against what we are unfree to do (Elster, 1983, pp.110–11). Moreover, the very exercising of our freedom shapes our wants – our current tastes depend very much upon our past choices. This is especially true of compulsive wants. In numerous ways, therefore, our experience of freedom determines our system of wants; freedom comes first, wants come second. To attempt to define freedom in terms of wants is, therefore, circular; it is defining freedom in terms of something that is the creature of freedom itself.

The wants theorist of freedom might reply to this criticism by arguing that the indisputable fact that wants are shaped by the circumstances within which we can exercise our freedom, and by the way in which we exercise it, does not mean that we must not *define* freedom in terms of wants. We can conceptualise freedom in terms of wants, notwithstanding the empirical fact that wants are shaped by the exercise of freedom; there is nothing circular in this. However, if our wants are entirely shaped by our restricted circumstances – if we are completely conditioned into developing some wants rather than others – it would seem odd to ignore this fact in an assessment of the extent of our freedom. Perhaps the answer is that the wants conception of freedom requires supplementation from the self-determination conception, in order to make clear that only those wants which are authentic to the agent contribute to her freedom.

The tenth and final criticism of the wants conception of freedom is that it makes freedom a highly contingent and relativistic concept. Since each person's set of wants is unique, what will constitute a loss of freedom to one person, because she is prevented from doing what she wants, will not constitute a loss of freedom to another person, because she is not prevented from doing what she wants. So the same obstacle which prevents two different people from doing the same thing is held to be a restriction on the freedom of one of them, but not of the other. This does not seem to be a satisfactory position to adopt, if only because it undermines comparative assessments of freedom. For example, on this view, country A where all civil liberties were suppressed but no one desired to have them, would be judged to be freer than country B where some civil liberties were protected but the population wanted more of them.

Conclusion on the doing what one wants conception of freedom

The attempt to characterise freedom in terms of doing what one wants is fraught with difficulties. The main problems centre around its essentially mental conception of freedom, raising questions about the notion of feeling free (is this notion a genuine or a spurious conception of freedom?); about what constitutes a want (is it any desire, or only certain desires, which entail freedom?); about wants which are in conflict (are some wants prior to others, and if so, does freedom consist in action in accordance with higher-order wants?); about the curtailing of desires (am I free if my desires are reduced to the point at which I no longer want to do things that I am unable to do?); about the autonomy of wants (is my freedom reduced if my wants are socially induced?); and about the relativity of wants (is X freer than Y if X's wants are less frustrated than Y's wants by the same restrictions?). However, since freedom implies action, and action implies desire (though desire does not necessarily imply action), it is difficult to avoid the conclusion that freedom has some connection with wants, even if the connection is not as close as the wants conception demands. This connection has, however, less to do with whether we *are* free or unfree, than with how much our various freedoms and unfreedoms *matter* to us.

7 Freedom as self-mastery

The conception of freedom as self-mastery arises out of dissatisfaction with the notion of freedom as doing what one wants.

> 'Freedom cannot be simply doing what one has a desire to do, for there is clearly such a thing as being the victim of a desire, of being a slave to a passion, of a desire's being irresistible and, hence, restricting one's freedom.' (Neely, 1974, p.37)

The self-mastery conception finds no difficulty in disposing of the paradox left unresolved by the wants conception, that renunciation of desires can increase freedom, since according to the self-mastery view, renunciation of desires is the key to freedom. The self-mastery conception concentrates even more than the wants and self-determination conceptions upon the personality of the agent, in the sense that it unambiguously locates the Y factor, the obstacle to freedom, within the mind of the agent herself. The Z factor, the objective, is portrayed as a target to be reached through a process of psychological struggle between the liberating and the enslaving elements within the agent's character (Maritain, 1942, p.639). The critical difference between the self-mastery conception and the self-determination conception, is that while the self-determination conception understands freedom to lie in control *by* the self, the self-mastery conception understands freedom to lie in control *over* the self. Although these two conceptions do share some ideas about freedom, self-determination essentially means autonomy, while self-mastery essentially means maturity.

There are many different formulations of the self-mastery view of freedom; I wish to examine the four most important formulations – moral virtue, personal development, intellectual rationality and mental stability. Although these formulations are not mutually exclusive – they do overlap in certain respects – they are sufficiently distinct in character to require separate identification and discussion.

(a) Moral virtue

This formulation of the self-mastery conception of freedom expresses the idea of a person overcoming the evil impulses in her nature. Doing as one wants is not liberty but licence. In Epictetus's words, 'we find no bad man free'. Or as Milton wrote, 'Licence they mean when they cry liberty, For he who loves that must first be good and wise'. Hartley Coleridge quaintly defined 'freedom, rightly understood' as 'a universal licence to be good'. The moral virtue version of the self-mastery view of freedom often takes on a spiritual form, 'Where the spirit of the Lord is', says St Paul, '*there* is liberty . . . for freedom did Christ set us free'. According to Calvin, if lust reigns and the flesh rules, we are in bondage to sin, from which we can only be liberated by faith in God's mercy. Submission to the will of God, then, is a necessary condition of freedom. 'O God ...whose service is perfect freedom' (Second Collect, Church of England Morning Prayer).

(b) Personal development

The second formulation of the self-mastery conception expresses the idea of a person fulfilling herself (Fromm, 1942, p.233). Green (1921, p.18) explains how 'the feeling of oppression which always goes along with the consciousness of unfulfilled possibilities', shows 'any kind of self-improvement as a demand for "freedom"'. Liberty, says Green (1911, pp.370-1), is not 'merely freedom to do as we like irrespectively of what it is that we like', but success in the resolve of people 'to make the most and best of themselves' in order to contribute to the common good. This reference to the common good indicates that Green has an objective view of what constitutes personal development. By contrast, for Gould ([C.C.], 1984, pp.89,91), the path to personal development is entirely subjective. Since freedom means 'self-development, that is, as a process of realising one's projects through activity in the course of which one forms one's own character and develops capacities', then, asks Gould, 'Who, other than the individual himself or herself, is to decide what capacities the individual is to develop freely, if the individual's development is to be self-development?'

(c) Intellectual rationality

The third formulation of the self-mastery thesis expresses the idea of a person making rational decisions. To be free, one must act, not on impulse, passion, whim or caprice, but in a purposeful, deliberate, reflective and disciplined fashion (Preston, 1982, p.74). Some thinkers, such as Plato, Locke and Leibnitz, prescribe the content of the pattern of conduct which exemplifies the rational truths of reason. Other writers, such as Dewey, interpret rationality in terms of applying one's intelligence to the issue at hand; i.e. in the trained power of thought, in turning things over in one's mind, in judiciously appraising evidence. This cerebral view of freedom is echoed by Knight (1941/2, p.95); 'the *primary* meaning of

freedom ... is *problem solving activity'*. It focuses attention less on
acting than on the process of thinking that goes on before action is
undertaken (Demos, 1942, pp.591–2).

(d) Mental stability

The final formulation of the self-mastery conception of freedom
expresses the idea of a person who is psychologically secure. Such a
person possesses a balanced, integrated personality, thinks and acts
in a sensible, self-aware fashion, and enjoys a feeling of inner
tranquillity and peace of mind. By contrast, a person who lacks
mental stability is in a condition of inner turmoil, strife, tension,
disorder, conflict, distraction or anguish. Such a person may be
labelled obsessional, neurotic, compulsive, infantile, inadequate,
abnormal or pathological, to indicate that her personality is out of
control, divided within itself, riven by internal conflict (Feinberg,
1980, p.9; Esheté, 1982, p.497). She is not her own master, since she
cannot help her behaviour (Dilman, 1961/2, p.47; McCloskey, 1965,
p.505). Freud's psychotherapeutic treatment was designed explicitly
to liberate patients from their neurotic symptoms, inhibitions and
abnormalities of character – to enable them, through self-knowledge,
to come to terms with who they were, and therefore to become free.

There are two general objections to all of these formulations of the
self-mastery conception of freedom. The first objection is the charge
that has been brought against both the self-determination and the
doing what one wants conceptions – that it reduces freedom to a
purely mental or cognitive state. It implies, for example, that
someone in a prison cell is free if she is in complete control of herself
emotionally. Lovelace expresses this implication with approval when
he asserts that 'Stone walls do not a prison make, Nor iron bars a
cage ... If I have freedom in my love, And in my soul am free.' It
also implies that we may increase our freedom simply by renouncing
our evil lusts, enervating impulses, undisciplined passions or mental
obsessions. The critics point out, however, that while it may be true
that in displaying such self-control, the prisoner and the reformed
person experience feelings of moral pride, or personal achievement,
or intellectual satisfaction, or mental relief, and that such feelings
may make them feel free, their objective conditions with respect to
freedom remain unaltered (Berlin, 1969, p.140).

The defender of the self-mastery conception of freedom could, however, reply to this charge by admitting that self-mastery is not *all* there is to liberty, but insisting that self-mastery represents one interpretation of the intrapersonal dimension of liberty, and an important and enduring interpretation at that. The self-possessed prisoner in a cell is obviously unfree in an interpersonal sense, but she may be free in an intrapersonal sense – liberated mentally from the oppressiveness of her incarceration. Her body is unfree, but her spirit or soul may be free. This seems to be a perfectly sensible way of conceptualising the notion of freedom, indicating once more that there is no single, correct conception of liberty; both interpersonal and intrapersonal conceptions matter if we are to gain a comprehensive grasp of its nature.

The second general objection to the self-mastery conception of freedom is, again, an objection that has been made to other conceptions – that it implies a sense in which people can be forced to be free. If, for example, coercion were successful in forcing someone to master her immoral appetites, damaging habits, unthinking instincts or neurotic drives, then she would be set free. Berlin (1969, p.134) has strongly criticised the self-mastery conception for this implication. However, defenders of the self-mastery thesis reject this criticism on the ground that a person *cannot* be forced to be self-masterful. Since self-mastery requires self-discipline, it is only the agent's own inner strength that can bring about self-mastery. All that external intervention can achieve is the creation of conditions under which freedom as self-mastery can be facilitated (Flathman, 1987, p.49). Green gives as an example of the proper role of the state the forbidding of voluntary contracts by which people enslave themselves to a master or subject themselves to debilitating working conditions imposed by an employer, since such contracts are degrading and prevent people from making 'the best of themselves' (Green, 1911, pp.372–3). Nevertheless, preventing people from disabling themselves from self-improvement may seem little different in practice from forcing people to improve themselves. If Green does not approve of forcing people to be free, he does seem to approve of forcing people not to be unfree. This is, however, a dilemma faced by virtually all conceptions of freedom – that in order to secure freedom in one sphere, steps may have to be taken which involve a reduction of freedom in another sphere.

We must now turn to particular criticisms that have been advanced separately against the four formulations.

(a) The *moral virtue* formulation has been criticised for confusing freedom with righteousness – i.e. a moral judgement on the use to which that freedom is put. It maintains that because an act is evil, therefore any person freely performing it is thereby rendered unfree. To many critics such as Steiner (1974/5, p.35) this is unintelligible: 'it is difficult to comprehend how one could perform an action which one ought not to perform – a wrong action – unless one is free to do it, not prevented from doing it'. It makes more sense to say that *X* is free to do the immoral act, but that if she does so, she behaves immorally. Writers who equate liberty with moral virtue are merely reinforcing their condemnation of immorality by labelling it as unfreedom (Dodds, 1957, p.16; Fosdick, 1939, p.88). As Bentham put it, 'is not liberty to do evil, liberty? If not, what is it?' To call a free act 'licence' is only to express an attitude of disgust towards it, not to prove that it is not a free act. What these critics are rightly saying is that interpersonal freedom is consistent with performing an immoral act. More controversially, Flathman claims that intrapersonal freedom is consistent with performing an immoral act. The error of the moral virtue account of freedom, says Flathman, is that it asserts that anyone who commits evil acts must be unfree, because acts of evil presuppose that the agent is enslaved to evil desires. But, says Flathman (1987, p.102), evil acts may well result from 'evaluations and choices' that are 'authentic to the actor as she is and as she understands herself and should not be regarded...as positive, internal constraints that compel movements and behaviours on the agent's "part"'. What the moral virtue theorists are doing is to divide the self into two parts, a real or true self, and an apparent or false self, and to say that when the latter prevails over the former I am unfree. But as Megone (1987, p.621) says, 'it is hard to see why I should now be identified with my "real" desires rather than the bundle of desires and emotions I actually possess'.

These critics have a point; it does seem unsatisfactory simply to equate either interpersonal or intrapersonal freedom with virtue. The moral virtue version of the self-mastery conception of freedom seems more convincing in situations where an agent is not just behaving immorally, but is resentful at her own failure to live up to her moral ideals. Here the picture of someone being a slave of her lusts makes sense – unlike the situation in which an immoral person feels no remorse, but enjoys her licentiousness: such a person does not seem so obviously to be unfree. Of course, from a religious viewpoint, a licentious person is enslaved by her sin, whether or not she feels remorse. But such a judgement presupposes acceptance of the spiritual doctrines underlying the religious viewpoint.

(b) The *personal development* formulation has been criticised for confusing freedom with self-realisation. Whether a person achieves self-realisation is one thing; whether she is free is another. For example, a person may be perfectly free to develop her talents, but fail to do so: she is free but not self-realised. Conversely, a person may realise her talents without being free to do anything else. Freedom, therefore, is not identical to self-realisation, nor is it a necessary means to self-realisation, though self-realisation may serve as 'one possible ... general *goal* or *purpose* of being free' (Weinstein, 1965, p.151). Nevertheless, a case could be made out for saying that in circumstances where the agent is oppressed by her failure to realise her potential, she may be said to experience a form of unfreedom.

(c) The *intellectual rationality* formulation has been criticised for confusing freedom with reason. Rational action, it is argued, does not entail any more freedom than does emotional action, though it may be wiser or more consistent action. If it is intelligible to say that rationality releases me from slavery to my emotions, it invites the reply that the result may be to enslave me to my reason. Singer ([M.G.], 1970, p.253) provides an amusing illustration of freedom from reason: 'There was once a cartoon ... in which two elegant matrons are depicted serving on a jury. One says to the other, "Oh, I never pay any attention to the evidence. I like to be free to make up my own mind"'. A person may be said to be imprisoned by her reason just as much as she may be said to be imprisoned by her emotions. 'Spinoza himself might be called a slave to his passion for utter rationality' (Muller, 1960, p.13). Too tight a rein held by reason over emotion may cramp and inhibit, rather than liberate, a person's personality. Only if the agent feels coerced by her emotions – feels herself at their mercy – is there a convincing sense of freedom in the idea of intellectual rationality, and only then if the agent does not feel coerced by her intellect. Of course, from an idealist standpoint like that adopted by Plato, there could be no question of reason 'cramping' a person's nature, since reason is the faculty that liberates the mind from error by unlocking the door to knowledge of the form of the good. But such a judgement presupposes acceptance of idealist metaphysics.

(d) Finally, the *mental stability* formulation has been criticised for confusing freedom with insight into oneself – self-knowledge. A person who is fully self-aware may well be a more balanced and integrated person, and as a result, perhaps, make better decisions than someone who acts unconsciously of her 'real' motives. But we would not say she was any freer, unless she experienced as a result of her self-knowledge a sense of liberation from oppressive mental torments. The mental stability version of self-mastery has also been criticised for reducing freedom to conformity. In so far as mental stability is interpreted as exhibiting itself in 'normal' behaviour, it gives rise to the suspicion that freedom lies in accepting the norms and standards of one's culture, and that the nonconformist is unfree. But the nonconformist may be freer than the conformist, in that she is exercising her mind in consciously rejecting the values of her society.

However, what of mentally disturbed persons, with whom the mental stability view of freedom is much concerned? These include people who have not consciously chosen an alternative lifestyle, since they are diagnosed as lacking the minimum degree of sanity to make real decisions. It does seem that such people are unfree in the sense that they are mentally disabled from acting freely. The view of psychiatrists such as Laing that the choices of the 'mentally-ill' are free but merely unorthodox or eccentric, does not seem entirely convincing. They may be free in the sense that they are not being externally coerced, but they are subject to internal drives over which they have no control. They are in the grip of their disease.

Conclusion on the self-mastery conception of freedom

This last point suggests that the central issue in the self-mastery characterisation of freedom lies in how we identify and where we locate the agent's 'self' – the 'X' factor (Feinberg, 1980, pp.8–9). If, for instance, we identify the self with our manifest drives, then whatever the stimulus of those drives, whether an illicit urge, a degrading impulse, an emotional reaction, or an obsessional compulsion, action in accordance with those drives is free. If, however, 'we take ourselves to live where our consciences are', then only when we resist those drives are we deemed to be free. In this respect, the self-mastery conception of freedom resembles both the self-determination conception and the doing what one wants characterisation, since both of these views of freedom raise the question of the identity of the agent's self. But it differs from the two other intrapersonal conceptions in that it is even less concerned than they are with the social dimension of liberty. It seems to treat the existence of fellow human beings as almost irrelevant to freedom. As such, it has been regarded as only a figurative or metaphorical conception of freedom – the purely mental obstacles with which it is almost exclusively concerned being interpreted as restraints on freedom only by analogy. However, a more considered and accurate appraisal of the self-mastery conception is that the internal obstacles with which it is concerned may be, in certain circumstances, perfectly real restraints on an agent's freedom, different in kind from external obstacles, but nonetheless authentic sources of one kind of unfreedom.

Conclusion on the conceptions of freedom

What are we to conclude from this extensive examination of the seven conceptions of freedom? I suggest that, while all of them have weaknesses in their interpretations of freedom, each of them captures some important aspect or dimension of that multi-textured concept. Our understanding of freedom does embrace in some measure each of the ideas of impedimentlessness, choice, power, citizenship, autonomy, want-satisfaction and self-control. There is little point in disputing which idea is the 'true' one, comprehensively embodying the essence of freedom, since none of them can reasonably lay claim to that prize – each is incomplete in itself. What may well be true, however, is that one conception is more appropriate than another conception when particular issues of freedom are under discussion. For example, in discussions of physical coercion, the most appropriate conception of freedom is likely to be that of absence of impediments; in discussions of consumerism, the most appropriate conception of freedom is likely to be that of availability of choices; in discussions of economic inequality, the most appropriate conception of freedom is likely to be that of effective power; in discussions of colonialism, the most appropriate conception is likely to be that of status; in discussions of socialisation, the most appropriate conception of freedom is likely to be that of self-determination; in discussions of paternalism, the most appropriate conception of freedom is likely to be that of doing what one wants; and in discussions of the human spirit, the most appropriate conception of freedom is likely to be that of self-mastery. In other words, we may legitimately make use of different conceptions of freedom in different contexts, since while the *concept* of freedom remains constant – in terms of X not being prevented by Y from doing or being Z – the most appropriate *conception* of freedom naturally varies as the issue under discussion focuses attention upon different aspects of the X, Y, and Z factors.

This is not to suggest that in any discussion involving liberty, only one conception of freedom will be appropriate; two or more conceptions may well be needed in order to clarify the issues of freedom raised. For instance, in discussions of paternalism, the self-determination conception may well be as relevant as the doing what one wants conception. Nor is it to suggest that the seven conceptions are entirely independent conceptions of freedom; on the contrary there are many points of contact between them, and they often serve to illuminate each other's contributions to our understanding of freedom. In this sense, they are complementary rather than competing conceptions of freedom. For instance, the power conception may be regarded as complementary to the impediments conception, adding to its insights, rather than replacing it. Nor, finally, is it to ignore the fact that the selection of one or other conception of freedom may well owe as much, if not more, to the value-judgements of the discussants as to the context of the issue under discussion. Indeed, the very decision as to which conception is most relevant to an issue may well reflect the values of the person making that decision. A person's attraction to a particular conception of freedom depends upon her view of what constitutes the X, Y and Z factors, and this in turn will frequently be connected to her opinions on wider questions of morality and ideology. This is one reason why, although the concept of freedom is not essentially-contested, any conception of that concept *is* essentially-contested, and it is also one reason why there is so much dispute over the meaning of freedom – people often seek to define freedom in such a way as to accommodate their differing views on society and human values.

3 Justifications for Freedom

Turning to the question of why freedom is valuable – i.e. why should we want to secure and protect freedom? – we are faced with the problem of deciding whether, given that there are, as I have suggested, seven different conceptions of the concept of freedom, we must examine arguments which seek to justify each of the seven conceptions in turn. On the face of it, it would seem an odd sort of justification that remained entirely agnostic between the seven conceptions, and could accommodate them all. Can we realistically expect, for example, that a justification for freedom defined as the absence of impediments would apply equally to freedom defined as self-mastery?

This problem may, however, be exaggerated. Many of the arguments used to justify freedom conceived in one sense *can* be used to justify freedom in another sense. For instance, the third of the six justificatory arguments which I examine in this chapter, that we have a *right* to freedom, could be used to justify freedom conceived in any of the seven senses: conferring upon people the right to be let alone; to have options open to them; to be in a position to exercise those options; to possess civil and political privileges; to be protected from social conditioning; to follow their own desires; and to pursue spiritual ends.

It is true, however, that some of the justificatory arguments fit in more appropriately with some, rather than with other, conceptions of freedom. For instance, the justificatory argument of autonomy is closely related to the conception of freedom as self-determination (though it may also underlie other conceptions), while the justificatory argument of utility is closely related to the conception of freedom as doing what one wants. In this chapter, however, I will assume that the six justificatory arguments can be adapted to apply

84

more or less generally to all or most of the seven conceptions of freedom, though most attention will be focused upon justifications for interpersonal freedom.

There are six attempts to justify freedom which I shall examine, namely the arguments of *presumption, neutrality, rights, autonomy, equality* and *utility*. First, the argument of presumption.

1 The presumption argument

The most immediate justification for freedom is that there is an initial or *prima facie* presumption in its favour. This justification has two alternative modes, a negative or procedural mode, and a positive or substantive mode. The negative or procedural mode of the presumption argument is that the burden of proof lies upon would-be restricters of freedom, not upon those faced with restrictions. Benn (1971, p.4) puts forward this view, claiming that 'a general liberty to do whatever one chooses unless someone else has good reasons for interfering to prevent it', is a 'fundamental principle in morals', and that the 'onus of justification . . . lies on the advocate of restraint, not on the person restrained'. If, for example, *A* decides to do something, and *B* decides to prevent her, it is for *B* to make out a case for his interfering with *A*, not for *A* to make out a case for her not being interfered with. Unless *B* can provide a justification for preventing *A*, *A* is free to go ahead; *she* does not need a reason (Benn, 1975/6, p.109). 'Absence of grounds for forbidding obliges one to permit' (Graham, 1965, p.64). Note that there is no assertion here that liberty is valuable in itself; all that is being claimed is that there is always a presumption in its favour. The legal principle of Habeas Corpus embodies this presumption, in that it requires the police to show why the detained person should not be released; it does not require the prisoner to show why she should be free (Benn and Peters, 1959, p.221).

However, none of these writers explain why this presumption should exist, or how it can be defended; they simply assert it. We might try to justify the presumption by making use of the notion of moral responsibility. According to Miller, as we saw in Chapter 2, a constraint on a person's freedom is properly defined as a restriction for which some other person bears a moral responsibility. Anyone who restricts another's freedom is therefore morally liable for doing so, and all moral liabilities must be defended. But no one bears a moral responsibility simply for exercising freedom, and so no one needs to justify being at liberty. However, this argument is not conclusive; it does not take care of the problem that rebuttal of a claim to interfere with a person's freedom does not in itself establish a claim to freedom on behalf of that person. Merely because *A*'s claim to interfere with *B*'s freedom is unsound, does not justify the presumption that *B* has a claim to freedom; all it shows is that *A*'s claim to interfere with that freedom is not justified. As Raz (1982, p.89) points out, this is 'a presumption of rationality and not of liberty'. That is to say, it is simply a demand that reasons must be given for any proposed interference. As such, it implies that reasons must also be given for liberty itself; i.e. that both unfreedom and freedom must submit to the test of rationality. Hence, implicit in the negative mode of the presumption justification, is an assertion that the positive value of liberty must be rationally established. Moreover, as Husak (1983, p.253) points out, the procedural presumption of freedom may be of comparatively little practical significance, since it cannot provide a means of *evaluating* any reason for coercion that a would-be interferer might advance. All that it demands is that a reason is given: *any* reason would therefore suffice.

This brings us to the positive or substantive mode of the presumption justification – the claim that there is a presumption in favour of freedom because liberty has intrinsic value (Hart, 1963, pp.21–2; Flathman, 1987, p.231; Berlin, 1969, p.169). The claim that freedom has intrinsic value implies that every free act, no matter how wicked, is good in at least one respect, that it is free (Mabbott, 1958, pp.62,76). But as Crocker (1980, p.119) points out, the very freedom of an evil act increases its wickedness. This suggests, as many writers have observed, that freedom in itself is neither good nor bad; whether freedom is valuable depends on the use to which it is put (Bergmann, 1977, p.100; Devlin, 1965, p.108; Muller, 1960, p.49; Somerville, 1962, p.289).

Perhaps the positive mode of the presumption justification of freedom might be taken to assert not that all freedoms are intrinsically valuable, since they are manifestly not, but that the act of exercising freedom is intrinsically valuable (Norman, 1987, p.37). This is the claim advanced by Dworkin ([G.], 1982, p.60); 'What does have intrinsic value is not having choices but being recognised as the kind of creature who is capable of making choices'. However, Dworkin's version of the presumption argument faces the question of what is intrinsically valuable about being recognised as a chooser. An answer to this question could be that being a chooser is a part of the human good – i.e. that the essence of being human is that one has the capacity to choose for oneself. This shifts the justification of freedom away from presumption to either autonomy, in that choosing is valued as a form of self-determination, or equality, in that choosing is valued as a mark of respect for human worth, and I consider below each of these notions (autonomy and equality) as separate justificatory arguments.

Conclusion on the argument of presumption

Neither the negative nor the positive mode of the presumption argument provides a satisfactory justification for freedom. The central weakness of the negative mode is that it fails to establish why the burden of proof rests exclusively on the restricter of freedom. There is no more justification for the advocate of freedom to occupy the high ground and to challenge the restricter to dislodge her, than there is for the restricter to occupy the high ground and to challenge the advocate of freedom to dislodge him. Suppose someone is walking along the street; the reason why we would not ask her to justify her freedom to do so is not because there is a presumption of freedom, but because we know that, in general, walking along the street is not forbidden. Suppose, however, she is walking on private land, or in a security area, or on shop premises at night, or along the street during a curfew; we *would be* justified in challenging her to defend herself – the onus would be on her to show what good reason she had for her perambulation. Husak (1983, p.359) gives another illustration – drawn from the practice of the United States Food and Drug Administration, which 'imposes the sensible policy that new drugs not be marketed while the evidence is insufficient to conclude whether the drug is harmful or safe. Here the presumption operates against freedom and in favour of coercion'. The positive mode of the presumption justification fails to remedy this deficiency in the negative mode, in that it cannot establish that freedom has intrinsic value, and therefore cannot demonstrate why it is that freedom advocates are entitled to occupy the high ground.

However, it may be that the presumption argument is not intended to serve as in itself a justification of freedom, but rather as a general format for such justifications. That is to say, every substantive argument seeking to justify freedom may be said to establish a formal presumption in favour of freedom, since someone who wanted to curtail freedom would then have to find reasons that were adequate to outweigh the argument advanced in its favour. In this sense, the value of the presumption argument lies less in the assertion that it offers an independent justification for freedom, than that it provides a formal structure or framework within which justificatory arguments operate. At any rate, what credibility the presumption argument does possess as a justification for freedom seems due to an implicit assumption within it that liberty has value either because it is a moral right, or because it is integrally related to some other moral value, such as autonomy, equality or utility. In the sections that follow, this implicit assumption will be explored, as each of these basic moral values is examined separately as a justification of freedom. But first we must turn to the second of the two attempts to defend freedom without apparently invoking basic moral values – the justification of freedom from the principle of neutrality.

2 The neutrality argument

If there is no presumption in favour of liberty, we may still be able to justify freedom without invoking basic moral values, by drawing on the principle of neutrality. Unlike the presumption argument, the neutrality argument is not employed to justify freedom *simpliciter*, but to provide us with a principle by which we can distinguish between justified and unjustified liberties. The principle of neutrality, according to Ackerman (1980, p.11), prescribes that no exercise of power over anyone can be justified if it 'requires the power-holder to assert: (a) that his conception of the good is better than that asserted by any of his fellow citizens, *or* (b) that, regardless of his conception of the good, he is intrinsically superior to one or more of his fellow citizens'. These two axioms are used to support the conclusion that we must be neutral between different persons and between different conceptions of the good, not favouring some at the expense of others. This entails that the only legitimate restriction that may be imposed upon anyone's freedom to pursue her conception of the good is to protect the like freedom of others to pursue *their* conception of the good. In other words, the principle of neutrality entails the principle of equal liberty (Jones, 1989a, p.31).

Five criticisms have been advanced against the neutrality principle as a means of distinguishing justified from unjustified liberties. The first is a criticism directed against the first of Ackerman's two basic axioms. While accepting the second axiom – that no-one is intrinsically superior to anyone else – Haksar rejects the first axiom – that no conception of the good is intrinsically superior to any other – on the grounds that 'some forms of life (such as the pursuit of truth and beauty) are intrinsically superior to other forms of life (such as a life devoted to the eating of one's excrement)'. Haksar (1979, pp.284,285,297) urges that 'the government should take such differences of worth into account', as a result of which 'the person who is practising the inferior form of life will get a worse deal... than the person who practises better forms of life'. He claims that such a breach of the equal liberty principle already operates in liberal democracies, in that 'forms of life, such as bestiality, nudism, eating one's own excrement... get only an inferior status in our society compared to the conventional forms of life'. However, Haksar does not explain why and on what criteria some life styles are to be judged intrinsically superior to others, nor does he satisfactorily explain why and when the government should discriminate in favour of them.

The second criticism of the neutralist justification of liberty is that even if the first axiom (that no conception of the good is intrinsically superior) is accepted, it does not follow from that axiom that all conceptions of the good must be tolerated. Suppose a society in which each conception of the good is given preference over every other conception of the good for one day in every year. There is no suggestion that the currently-enforced conception of the good is superior to any other conception; it is currently-enforced merely because it exists in the society and can therefore claim equally with every other conception a period of time in which it is to be enforced.

The truth of the matter is that the first axiom is either a statement of fact or a moral claim. If it is interpreted as a statement of fact – i.e. that different conceptions of the good exist – then toleration of these conceptions is only justified if we add a moral principle that people who hold different conceptions of the good are entitled to act

on them. But where does this moral principle come from? Perhaps
Rawlsian rational choice theory can help, in that it could be argued
that it would be rational for people in the original position to
choose toleration, given the known fact of diversity of conceptions
of the good. But this ignores the problem of intensity of attachment
to different conceptions of the good. For example, it might be
rational behind Rawls's veil of ignorance to choose Sabbatarian
legislation, if one knew that religious preferences for Sabbatarianism were generally stronger than were secular preferences against
Sabbatarianism.

If the first axiom is interpreted as a moral statement,
incorporating the principle that people are entitled to act on their
conceptions of the good because one person's moral system is as
good as another's, then the problem of deriving an 'ought' from an
'is' disappears, since here the 'ought' is being derived from an
'ought'. But how can a neutralist argue that one moral system is as
good as another, without abandoning neutralism? Indeed, the
assertion that one moral system is as good as another does not make
sense even if uttered by a non-neutralist. 'Could, for example, a
Christian who admitted that other religious/moral positions were
just as good as Christianity still be regarded as a Christian?'
(Harrison, 1975/6, p.133).

The neutralist might, however, follow Rawls and Dworkin [R.]
and claim that the first axiom incorporates a moral statement of a
different kind – not that all conceptions of the good are of equal
merit, but that all persons, as beings capable of adopting a
conception of the good, merit equal respect. In effect, this claim
supports axiom one by invoking the substance of axiom two – that
no person can legitimately claim to be superior to any other person.
Such a claim is a strong one, since to refute it would entail
embracing a full-blooded form of perfectionism, which is very
difficult to defend.

The third criticism of the neutralist justification of liberty,
however, is an accusation that the neutralists themselves covertly
embrace a perfectionist moral judgement in favour of toleration.
The critics argue that the neutralist justification of liberty is not
wholly neutralist, since by endorsing a particular conception of the
ideal form of human life – one that embraces the ideal of toleration –
it implicitly incorporates within it an element of perfectionism
(Hare, 1963, p.177). This criticism is sometimes expressed in terms

of the charge that the neutrality principle *cannot* be neutral about neutrality – it cannot tolerate the intolerant. Since it is wedded to the two axioms – that no conception of the good, and no person, can be held to be superior to any other – the neutrality principle *cannot* deal neutrally with any sexist, racist or perfectionist ideas that deny either of the two axioms. It must suppress such ideas. However, Jones (1989, p.27) defends the neutrality principle against this charge, on the ground that there is nothing inconsistent in a neutral state refusing to tolerate anti-neutral views; this 'does not undermine its claim to be neutral', but 'merely indicates where it takes its stand'. The neutral state does not have to be a neutral broker amongst competing views on the issue of neutrality itself. 'Just as democrats do not have to be "democratic" about democracy, so neutralists do not have to be neutral about neutrality'. In defending itself from attack by the intolerant, a neutralist state is, of course, acting in an intolerant way, and in this respect neutralism entails an element of unfreedom. But the neutrality principle is not designed to justify *every* freedom, but rather to distinguish between legitimate and illegitimate freedoms. Hence the 'criticism' that the neutrality principle does not tolerate the intolerant, turns out to be not a criticism properly-called at all, but a clarification of the nature of the principle.

However, one implication of neutralism's intolerance of the intolerant, is that it favours individualistic over communalistic life-styles. This is the fourth criticism of the neutralist justification of liberty – that it is inherently slanted towards individualistic conceptions of the good. In so far as communalistic groups threaten the liberty of their members to pursue their own conceptions of the good in their own way, the neutral state must interfere with such groups in order to protect each individual's personal choice of life-style. Moreover, even when there is no explicit attempt on the part of a neutral state to favour individualistic over communalistic conceptions of the good – i.e. in circumstances where all members of communalistic groups freely choose their collectivist life-style – discrimination against communalistic conceptions of the good, it is alleged by the critics, will be the inevitable outcome of a policy of state neutralism. That is to say, if neutralism is interpreted as enjoining that no one shall be prevented from pursuing their conception of the good, then it is inevitable that individualistic conceptions of the good will thrive, whilst communalistic conceptions of the good will decline, possibly to the point of atrophy, because individualistic conceptions of the good are more easily pursued than are communalistic conceptions of the good, since they are cheaper and they require less cooperation from other people. Raz (1986, pp.119–20) criticises Rawls on this score.

Jones (1989a, pp.22–3) defends the neutralists against this charge, arguing that since there is no suggestion in Rawls's theory that the more successful conceptions of the good are being *deliberately* favoured because they are superior to the less successful, there is nothing here that is inconsistent with neutralism. But critics such as Raz insist that neutralism cannot ignore such inadvertent outcomes, but must positively strive to ensure that everyone can pursue their conception of the good, whether that conception is individualistic or communalistic. 'The state can be neutral only if it creates conditions of equal opportunities for people to choose any conception of the good, with an equal prospect of realising it' (Raz, 1986, p.124). This may entail state intervention to protect threatened life-styles (individualistic or communalistic) from extinction by neglect or indifference. 'A single generation of atheists should not be permitted to transform all Christian shrines into parking lots' (Ackerman, 1980, p.217). It may even imply state intervention to protect 'other, incipient, forms of life that may arise' (Weale, 1983b, p.9).

However, the attempt to avoid deliberate and/or inadvertent discrimination against communalistic conceptions of the good faces formidable difficulties. For example, what does 'equal promotion of conceptions of the good' entail? How can we know whether everyone's prospect of realising their conception of the good has been 'equalised'? Is it when everyone is equally satisfied? If so, 'what if some individuals choose goals which are intrinsically less satisfying than others?' (Jones 1989a, p.15). Moreover, how can a government begin to identify what future conceptions of the good may arise in order to provide equal promotion for them?

The fifth criticism of the neutralist justification of freedom is that neutralism cannot deal neutrally with conflicts between mutually exclusive conceptions of the good. The neutrality principle protects each person's liberty to pursue her concept of the good only up to the point where it threatens the like liberty of anyone else to pursue their conception of the good. This is the reason why the neutrality principle cannot tolerate life-styles of communities beyond the point at which they remove the liberty of their community members to choose their own life styles. But how can the neutrality principle deal with situations in which one conception of the good *can only be pursued at all* at the expense of another conception of the good?

Giving the example of an embittered ex-husband who is hell-bent on assaulting his ex-wife, Ackerman argues that the neutralist state must protect the ex-wife, not because her conception of the good is intrinsically superior to that of her ex-husband, nor because she is intrinsically superior to him, but because citizens in a liberal community must eschew force and use only 'dialogic' – i.e. verbal – means of settling disputes. However, if the state protects the ex-wife from the ex-husband, it is discriminating in favour of her or her conception of the good, since it is ruling that the aggressed person's freedom must take precedence over the aggressor's freedom. Such a ruling is no more neutralist than is the opposite decision – to allow the ex-husband freedom to assault his ex-wife – since both rulings entail giving priority to one person, or one conception of the good, over another.

The neutralist might reply that the reason why the ex-husband ought to be restrained is because his conception of the good involves imposing external preferences on his ex-wife (by requiring that she is available for assault), whereas his ex-wife's conception of the good only involves personal preferences (she merely wants to be left alone). But, indirectly, the ex-wife *is* imposing external preferences on her ex-husband, in that she is requiring that his pursuit of his conception of the good is frustrated. Hence both ex-husband and ex-wife have conceptions of the good which can only be pursued at the expense of the other's conception of the good.

The neutralist might, however, argue that the neutral state is not obliged to be neutral between harmful and harmless conceptions of the good. 'Although committed to being neutral between opera lovers and rock concert lovers, the neutral state is not committed to displaying neutrality with respect to arsonists or rapists' (Mendus, 1989, p.118). In other words, there are limits which neutralism imposes upon itself; it does not demand that the neutral state must be neutral concerning *anything* that people might consider to be part of their conception of the good. Indeed, neutralists generally follow Mill in claiming that there are boundaries around each person within which that person has a sovereign right. On this assumption, the ex-husband would be judged to be intruding into the ex-wife's rightful area of immunity, but the ex-wife would be judged not to be intruding into the ex-husband's rightful area of immunity. Hence protecting the ex-wife from the ex-husband is a matter of the 'right' rather than the 'good'. However, such a defence of neutralism is an admission that it is an incomplete justification of freedom, since in certain circumstances its application requires an additional principle – in this example, Mill's harm principle.

The neutralist could, perhaps, argue that such issues of conflict between mutually exclusive conceptions of the good can be resolved by employing a neutral procedure, such as democratic decision-making by majority vote, to determine which conception(s) of the good should prevail over other(s). But this could simply mean that the majority's conception of the good would prevail. Neutral procedures do not guarantee neutral outcomes. Even *unanimity* of opinion about the right priority between conflicting conceptions of the good would not mean that in favouring one over another, the government was acting neutrally; it would only mean that it was acting uncontroversially.

Since the principle of neutrality faces this fifth criticism wherever there is conflict between mutually exclusive conceptions of the good, it is a serious matter for the neutralist argument. Note that such conflict may arise not only between individualistic conceptions, but also between communalistic conceptions themselves, and between individualistic and communalistic conceptions, in circumstances where a communalistic conception could only be pursued in an environment in which alien conceptions of the good had been suppressed.

Conclusion on the argument of neutrality

There are three difficulties with the neutralist justification of freedom. First, neutralism contains within it a moral claim that people should be equally free to pursue their own conceptions of the good. Hence the neutrality principle is not self-justifying; it requires justification by some principle of right. But this implies that the real basis of the justification of freedom is not, after all, the principle of neutrality, but the principle of right which lies behind it. The question then arises, why not justify freedom by appeal directly to this principle of right itself? This is the mode of justification considered in the next section. The second difficulty with the neutralist justification of freedom is the fact that it cannot justify freedom *simpliciter*, since it does not defend the freedom of the intolerant. This difficulty is, however, not so much a criticism as a clarification, because the neutrality principle does not seek to justify freedom *per se*; it seeks to serve as a criterion for distinguishing legitimate liberties from illegitimate liberties. The third difficulty is the problem that the neutrality principle faces in trying to deal neutrally with all the different conceptions of the good that exist in society, many of which compete with one another, and some of which are mutually exclusive. It seems that the neutrality principle is unable to distinguish between legitimate and illegitimate liberties, without the aid of some other moral value (such as Mill's harm principle, or the principle of democracy).

3 The rights argument

I have argued that it is not possible to justify freedom *simpliciter* by invoking either the notion of presumption or the notion of neutrality, and that, indeed, these notions are properly interpreted not as general justifications of freedom, but as, respectively, a format into which such justifications can be framed, and a rule for favouring some freedoms over others. As such, each of these notions needs to be supported by substantive moral argument, since whatever force they do have in defending freedom is due to the fact that implicit in both is some form of moral assertion. In the rest of this chapter I examine the four main moral claims that have been put forward to justify freedom – rights, autonomy, equality and utility.

The claim that people have a right to liberty has been made frequently. A typically bald assertion of this right is made by Aiken (1962, p.311):

'The moral foundation of liberty . . . is nothing other than the right to be at liberty itself. In short, the fountainhead of freedom . . . is not utility but simply and solely the principle that every person has a right to be at liberty. This principle . . . requires justification by no other principle whatever.'

Day (1987, p.127) states that the reason why 'all restraint, *qua* restraint, is an evil', is because 'all acts of restraint violate the general moral right to liberty'.

What is the basis upon which this assertion of a right to freedom rests? Hart (1967, p.53) has proposed the conditional justification that 'if there are any moral rights at all, it follows that there is at least one natural right, the equal right of all men to be free'. This is because to have a right entails having a moral justification for limiting the freedom of another person, and this in turn entails the equal right to freedom held by that other person. Let me explain Hart's argument by using an illustration. Suppose I have a claim right to the fruits of my labour; the assertion of such a right necessarily entails that everyone else must refrain from interfering with that right of mine – i.e. that everyone else's freedom is restricted. But this in turn implies that everyone else has a right to freedom in the first place, since if everyone else did *not* have a right to freedom in the first place, there would be no need for me to assert my right to the fruits of my labour – there would be no need to *justify* any restriction on everyone else's freedom.

Hart's argument is open to criticism on four grounds. First, it is purely hypothetical in character, claiming that *if* there are any moral rights, then the right to freedom must be one of them. But if there are no moral rights, then the argument fails to get off the ground. Hart himself does not assert that there are any moral rights, only that there are moral duties. But Steiner claims that moral duties necessarily entail moral rights. For example, the injunction 'thou shalt not steal' is not intelligible unless there is some conception of property rights. Hence if there are any moral duties – i.e. if there is any morality – then there are moral rights. Of course, the argument is still hypothetical in the sense that it presupposes that morality exists. Moreover, it is possible to argue, *pace* Steiner, that not all duties entail corresponding rights and, more controversially, that there can be, and have been, rightless moralities (for example, some theocentric moralities).

The second criticism of Hart's argument is that it only serves to justify particular freedoms, not freedom in general. For instance, from the assertion that I have a claim-right to the fruits of my labour, and that everyone else has a corresponding duty to refrain from interfering with that right, it does not follow that everyone has a natural right to freedom in general which is here being restricted in one particular respect; all that follows is that everyone has a natural right to one particular freedom which is here being restricted – the freedom to appropriate commodities. However, Steiner (1974, p.201) argues convincingly that it does not make sense to claim a particular right against other people, unless we recognise these other people as moral agents; and recognising people as moral agents means endowing them with the right to freedom in general.

The third criticism of Hart's argument for a general right to freedom is that it fails to rule out the possibility of unequal freedoms. Harris gives the example of a Nazi denial that Jews are moral agents; for the Nazi, only Aryans are moral agents, and they have no moral duty to respect the freedom of non-moral agents such as Jews. The reply of Hart and Steiner to this criticism is to argue that people like the Aryans who regard themselves as an exclusive élite, cannot claim any *moral right* to override the claims of Jews, because if the Jews are excluded from equal rights, they have no *moral duty* to obey the Aryans or to respect their rights (if the Jews have such duties, they must be moral agents, and therefore entitled to equal liberty with all other moral agents, including Aryans). Harris has suggested, however, that Aryans could argue that their rights over the Jews are not claim-rights – i.e. rights which presuppose corresponding moral duties on the part of the Jews – but liberty-rights in the Hobbesian 'state of nature' sense of a 'right to all things' – i.e. liberties which do not imply duties on the part of Jews (Harris, [N.G.E.], 1972, p.126). But it is claim-rights with which the Aryans are concerned – i.e. rights which Jews have no right to breach. Merely to demand liberty-rights is to concede that Jews are under no obligation to respect them.

The fourth criticism of the justification of freedom in terms of rights is that advanced by Dworkin, to the effect that any assertion of a general right to freedom could only be sustained at the cost of diluting the content of that right to the point of insignificance. In a sense similar to the above distinction between liberty rights and claim rights, Dworkin distinguishes between weak and strong rights to liberty. A weak right to liberty may be founded upon the basis that someone wants it, or that it would be good for him to have it. 'In this sense', says Dworkin ([R.], 1978, pp.268,269), 'I would be prepared to concede that citizens have a right to liberty. But in this sense I would also have to concede that they have a right, at least generally, to vanilla ice cream'. Such a notion hardly does justice to the strength of the claim of a right to liberty demanded by rights theorists, since it is such a trivial claim that it could be legitimately overruled by even a small advantage to the public interest. A strong right to liberty entails that a citizen is entitled to it, and that 'it is wrong for the government to deny it to him even though it would be in the general interest to do so'. But if we adopt this stronger sense of right, no general right to freedom *can* exist, since it would imply that every restriction imposed by government was an infringement of the right to liberty. Dworkin gives the example of the government imposing a one-way traffic flow down Lexington Avenue, arguing that in doing so, the government did not violate anyone's right to liberty, since no one had a right to drive up Lexington Avenue in the first place.

However, Dworkin may be overstating his case. It could be argued that there *is* a prima facie right to travel up Lexington Avenue, even though it is a very weak right – there are alternative roads to use – and as such may be overruled legitimately by a small gain to the public interest. This does not devalue the notion of a general right to liberty, since we can accept that distinctions must be drawn between weaker rights (i.e. those overruled by small gains to the public interest), and stronger rights (those not overruled by small gains to the public interest), without abandoning the assertion of a general right to liberty. Only if the rights theorist were to insist that rights were absolutely inviolate – i.e. that no amount of public interest could ever be allowed to overrule them – would this argument be unsatisfactory.

Nevertheless, defending the rights argument along these lines entails the difficulty of finding some means of making the distinction between weaker and stronger rights. Dworkin argues that such a distinction must be founded upon either a qualitative or a quantitative basis. If we use a qualitative basis, we must explain why, for example, we have a right to free speech, but not a right to drive cars down Lexington Avenue, in terms of some human quality, such as autonomy, for which free speech is essential, but for which driving down Lexington Avenue is not. But any such explanation is open to empirical refutation, in that the liberty of free speech may not actually enhance everyone's autonomy, while the liberty of driving down Lexington Avenue may be an important form of autonomy for some people. Of course, we may simply ignore the latter sort of person – on the grounds that their reaction is an idiosyncratic and aberrant response to a restriction which has no real relevance to autonomy – and take the view that, in general, free speech enhances autonomy more than does driving up Lexington

Avenue. But this is to assert a controversial judgement about the conditions of autonomy, as Dworkin points out (1978, p.271). In any case, the basis of the justification of liberty will have shifted from freedom as a matter of rights, to freedom as a condition of autonomy, an argument which we consider in the next section. If we use a quantitative basis to distinguish between weaker and stronger rights to freedom, we must explain why/how the less important freedoms contain fewer units of freedom than are contained in the more important freedoms. But any such explanation faces a barrage of objections – which are discussed in the next chapter, on the measurement of freedom.

Conclusion on the argument of rights

There are two problems faced by any assertion that there is a general right to liberty. First, such an assertion depends upon the assumption that all moral agents possess the right to liberty but this assumption cannot be taken for granted. Second, the rights theorist must establish some convincing way of distinguishing between less important and more important rights to liberty, since otherwise she would be committed to the unworkable view that all rights to liberty are inviolate – i.e. that everyone has an inviolate right to do anything. But a distinction between less important and more important rights to liberty cannot be made without employing some moral value other than that of rights (such as autonomy), and thereby shifting the basis of the justification of freedom from the notion of rights.

Perhaps, however, it is a mistake to seek to interpret the rights justification of liberty as a self-sufficient argument for freedom. It may be argued that the right to freedom is in itself not a justification for freedom, but a claim about the moral standing of any demand for freedom – a claim which must be substantiated by reference to some set of moral values independent of the notion of rights. Hence, for example, if on grounds of, say autonomy, we are held to be entitled to exercise some freedom, we are deemed to have a *right* to that freedom. The right to liberty is thus the consequence of a prior justificatory argument for freedom. In this sense, the rights justification would resemble the presumption justification, serving as a format into which justificatory arguments can be presented, rather than a justificatory argument *per se*. In any event, the rights

justification of freedom, like both the presumption and neutralist
justifications, is incomplete as it stands, requiring substantiation
from other values. One such other value is that of autonomy, to
which we now turn.

4 The autonomy argument

The autonomy argument seeks to justify liberty in terms of the
supposed good of being ruled by oneself. As such, it raises an
immediate problem for our analysis; since autonomy is widely
regarded as being synonymous with self-determination – both entail
the idea of living in accordance with one's own values – the
autonomy justification is in danger of circularity. That is to say, if
we adopt the conception of freedom as self-determination, then we
would be justifying self-determination as a means to self-
determination. To avoid this circularity, I propose to separate the
discussion of the autonomy justification into two parts: first, to look
at the arguments from autonomy for freedom conceived *not* as self-
determination, but as the absence of impediments; and, second, to
look at the arguments for justifying autonomy itself – i.e. as freedom
conceived in terms of self-determination. I begin with the first part
of this discussion.

One of the most widely-rehearsed justificatory arguments for
liberty is that freedom from restrictions is valuable, even
indispensable, for human autonomy (Lindley, 1986, pp.8–9; Raz,
1986, p.400). We need liberty from restrictions if we are to carry out
our plans of life; as purposive beings, we have the capacity for
autonomy, but unless we are allowed the freedom to exercise this
capacity, we will never be in control of our lives (Jones, 1989b, p.64).

The assumption that freedom from restriction is essential for
autonomy – has, however, been much criticised. For one thing,
freedom from restriction is not a sufficient condition for autonomy
(Weale, 1983a, p.59). I may have such freedom, but I will not behave
in an autonomous way in making use of that freedom if, for
example, in my actions I am always 'mindlessly mimicking the
tastes, opinions, ideals, goals, principles, or values of others'
(Young, 1986, p.8). This is a familiar point – that the agent must
not only be free, but be exercising that freedom independently.
However, the matter is more complex than this, since the capacity

for exercising freedom independently – the capacity for autonomy –
is dependent upon external circumstances, in that it needs to be
learned (Feinberg, 1980, p.26). As Mendus (1989, p.96) puts it, 'the
development of autonomy requires proximity to the world – it
requires that the agent learn and develop his autonomy within an
environment and against a background supportive of that ideal'. We
cannot become autonomous on our own (Dworkin, [G.], 1976,
p.24). This observation raises the conceptual question of whether
autonomy that is socially-learned can be defined as autonomy; if we
are socialised into autonomy are we really autonomous? The
autonomy theorist could answer this question in the affirmative by
noting that autonomy does not entail that we possess the capacity to
determine whether we are autonomous creatures, but only that we
possess the capacity to make choices which are authentically our
own, and that this is compatible with socially-learned autonomy.
Nevertheless, it is clear that in order to become autonomous, we
must submit to certain restrictions upon our liberty (Scruton, 1983,
p.193). Moreover, these restrictions may have to be permanent,
since our capacity for autonomy may never be fully developed, and
even fully-developed autonomous agents must be protected from
threats posed to their autonomy. Indeed, Mendus (1989, p.94)
argues that if autonomy is interpreted (as it is by many writers) as
rational self-determination, 'unlimited interference may be justified
in the name of the promotion of autonomy'.

This conclusion, that the development and maintenance of
autonomy entails significant restrictions on freedom, is acknowledged by proponents of autonomy such as Raz (1986, p.424), who
notes that the autonomy principle would justify 'taking action to
assimilate' non-autonomous groups, such as tightly-knit ethnic
communities into an autonomous culture. Young (1986, p.5) and
Husak (1981) argue that certain paternalistic policies are necessary
to enhance autonomy, while Flathman (1987, pp.219–20) claims
that there is a fundamental tension in liberalism between the
principle of autonomy and the principle of freedom from
restrictions. It does seem that in some important respects autonomy
demands unfreedom.

However, the weight of this conclusion should not be exaggerated.
The fact that, in some circumstances, autonomy demands limitation
upon freedom should not obscure the fact that, for the most part,
autonomy entails freedom from restriction. The autonomy principle,

like the neutrality and rights principles, is properly interpreted as a selective, rather than an undiscriminating, justification for freedom; it endorses only those freedoms from restriction that enhance autonomy. But the extent of such freedoms may be quite considerable.

The second part of the discussion of the autonomy justification is concerned with the claim that autonomy is itself a form of freedom – interpreting freedom as self-determination – and as such is a valuable human good. Autonomy theorists have suggested four reasons why we should regard autonomy – and, therefore, freedom as self-determination – as valuable. Raz (1986, p.394) argues that 'The value of personal autonomy is a fact of life. Since we live in a society whose social forms are to a considerable extent based on individual choice...we can prosper in it only if we can be successfully autonomous'. But this is merely a truism: that it is best to be autonomous if we live in an autonomous culture. The real issue is – is it best to live in an autonomous culture in the first place? Is autonomy itself necessarily a good thing?

Rawls argues that rational agents choosing principles of justice under the veil of ignorance would opt for institutions that protected autonomy, because everyone has an interest in being autonomous. However, Haksar (1979, p.180) disputes this argument, on the ground that we cannot take it for granted that everyone has an interest in being autonomous. 'The worst off...may be better off in a non-autonomous society where they have been suitably conditioned than they would be in an autonomous society'. There are distinct advantages in being heteronomous, including 'increased psychological security as a result of not having the burdens of choice'. Are such advantages necessarily of less weight to people than the advantages conferred on them by living in an autonomous society in which they are able to choose for themselves their form of life? In itself rational choice theory cannot tell us whether autonomy is preferable to heteronomy, since the preference depends upon what kind of person we happen to be, and people in the Rawlsian original position are ignorant concerning their own personalities.

If, however, a perfectionist ideal is injected into the rational choice theory, then autonomy will become preferable to heteronomy, because it is a condition of human good. This is the third suggested reason for valuing autonomy – that autonomy is an integral part of the good life, of intrinsic value to its possessor, enhancing personal dignity and self-esteem (Young, 1986, p.26). However, to say that autonomy is of intrinsic value is to imply that an act of choice is itself valuable, irrespective of what it is that is chosen. But as Jones (1989b, p.65) observes, 'if the content of an individual's aims in life is of so little consequence, it becomes puzzling why his choice over those aims should be of such all-consuming importance'. The perfectionist view entails that every act that is performed autonomously, no matter how evil its consequences, is good in at least one respect, that it was undertaken autonomously. But the fact that an evil act has been undertaken autonomously increases rather than reduces the evil therein (Young, 1986, p.31; Raz, 1986, p.412). Moreover, the perfectionist view of autonomy implies that autonomy is part of everyone's conception of the good life. But in heteronomous communities such as Muslim societies, autonomy is far from being an ingredient of the good life – on the contrary, it may be a threat to the good life.

The fourth suggested reason for valuing autonomy is that autonomy, if not itself part of the good life (intrinsically good), is a means to the attainment of the good life (consequentially good). That is to say, autonomy makes people better off. But does it? Ladenson (1975, p.34) points out that autonomous choices may be of 'extremely poor quality... ignorant, narrow minded, uncreative, self-deceptive, weak willed'. The autonomy theorist could, however, reply to this charge by arguing that while, of course, autonomous decisions may not always turn out for the best, there is no guarantee that heteronomous decisions will always turn out for the best. Moreover, the fact that autonomous choices are made by ourselves is itself a prime source of well-being, since we resent other people making decisions for us, and we take considerable satisfaction in reaching our own decisions. But a persuasive rebuttal of this reply is that the satisfaction taken by the agent in the exercise of her autonomy could be artificially manufactured in a manipulated, non-autonomous environment, where only the feeling or appearance of autonomy is secured. Huxley's *Brave New World* constituted just such a situation of apparent, but illusory, autonomy. (Young, 1986, pp.22–3). However, Crocker (1980, p.117) argues that the value an agent gains from her autonomy depends critically upon the fact that her autonomy is genuine, not counterfeit.

'It is rational to want to have an excellence ... rather than simply to have the appearances, even if the appearances are perfect and there is no danger that we will be disabused of our beliefs. Not to care whether one actually has an excellence, so long as one thinks one does, is an odd attitude to adopt towards oneself.'

Nozick (1974, p.43) similarly claims that 'we want to *do* certain things and not just have the experience of doing them', and that 'what *we are* is important to us'. Why, Nozick asks, 'should we be concerned only with how our time is filled, but not with what we are?' However, this leaves unanswered the question of how we can ever know whether our autonomy is genuine or spurious if 'the appearances are perfect'? Like Megone (1987, p.616), Crocker (1980, p.117) answers this question by claiming that, in practice, the illusion of autonomy will eventually be exposed, and so 'the only workable way to have the appearance of freedom for any length of time ... is really to have freedom'. But of course this is an empirical claim, and may be challenged by evidence of closed societies that have sustained the illusion of autonomy for generations. In any case, this attempt to justify freedom interpreted as self-determination on grounds that autonomy promotes well-being, shifts the basis of the justification away from autonomy towards utility.

Conclusion on the argument of autonomy

The connection between liberty and autonomy is not a simple and straightforward one. In the first place, freedom conceived as absence of impediments is not a sufficient condition of autonomy, and there is some doubt as to whether it is always a necessary condition, since the very capacity for autonomy demands certain systematic and permanent restrictions on freedom. It is more convincing to claim, not that interpersonal freedom *in general* is justified by autonomy, but that *some* interpersonal liberties are a logical pre-requisite of autonomy. Moreover, even this modified claim may be challenged by asking which particular freedoms are necessary for autonomy. Raz (1986, p.410) observes that no such case can be made out categorically, since the significance of options to a person's autonomy depends on the circumstances of that person's culture. In the second place, the value of autonomy as itself a form of freedom (self-determination) is problematical, in that the assertion of its intrinsic value must face the fact that some autonomous acts may be evil. The assertion that autonomy has consequential value is challenged both by the fact that autonomous agents may sometimes choose unwisely, and by the fact that the feeling of autonomy could be manufactured in a non-autonomous environment.

However, these criticisms of the autonomy justification are only fatal to an exaggerated or extreme version of it. Interpreted more moderately, it would seem to justify some freedoms, since *some* freedoms undoubtedly contribute to the development of autonomy, and self-determination (autonomy as a conception of freedom) is *in some respects* undoubtedly a human good. We must now turn to the fifth justification of freedom – that freedom is entailed by the principle of equality.

5 The equality argument

Ronald Dworkin (1978) is the main proponent of the equality justification of freedom, arguing that, although there is no general right to liberty, certain liberties have the status of rights (in the strong sense) because they are underpinned or entailed by 'the principle of equal concern and respect'. According to Dworkin, only those freedoms which are deemed necessary to maintain the right of equal concern and respect are sacrosanct: other freedoms may be unobjectionable, even desirable, but they do not have the status – the moral weight – of the 'strong' liberties. Applying this test, Dworkin concludes, for example, that we cannot object to restrictions imposed upon the direction of traffic along Lexington Avenue, since no-one's right to equal concern and respect is thereby violated. But we can object to restrictions imposed upon newspaper editors who are critical of the government, since such restrictions violate the right to equal concern and respect; it is an affront to human dignity to have one's opinions censored simply because they embarrass the government. Like most of the other justification arguments, therefore, the argument from equality does not attempt a justification of freedom in general, but only a justification for particular liberties. Indeed, on the equality test, a great number of restrictions on liberty would be legitimate, provided that they could be shown to promote the public interest without impinging on anyone's right to equal concern and respect.

Dworkin's principle of equal concern and respect has, however, been much criticised. The central criticism is that it is a highly subjective principle. Whether or not a particular restriction on liberty is a violation of the principle of equal concern and respect seems to be a matter of opinion. For example, Dworkin's defence of the anti-Vietnam war demonstrators who wore badges bearing the slogan 'Fuck the Draft', was based on the view that dissenters must be allowed to convey their sense of outrage in terms that matched their feelings. It 'is arrogant of the majority to suppose that the orthodox methods of expression are the proper ways to speak, for this is a denial of equal concern and respect' (Dworkin, [R.], 1978, p.201). But, says Haksar (1979, p.268), what about the right to equal concern and respect of the 'timid old lady in Chicago' who is upset by such language? 'The view that the demonstrators express their personality when they use obscene words, whereas the old lady's need for peace and quiet is of a lower order of importance, seems to express a perfectionist judgement.' Dworkin's position expresses his own value judgements as to whose respect is more important; a different set of value judgements would yield a different conclusion about the implications of the principle of equal concern and respect.

Dworkin attempts to meet this criticism by distinguishing between 'personal' and 'external' preferences, and requiring that the latter are ignored in the application of his equality principle. A 'personal' preference is a preference that someone possesses to act in a particular way. An 'external' preference is a preference that someone possesses for other people to act in a particular way. Dworkin's argument is that as a general rule of thumb, only those policy decisions which are based purely on calculations of personal preference will be in conformity with the principle of equal concern and respect. If external preferences are also taken into account, then some people could be treated as a means to the satisfaction of other people's ends, and thereby their right to equal concern and respect would be violated. The reason why we cannot accept the timid old lady's veto on the language used by anti-Vietnam war demonstrators is because that would entail taking external preferences into account.

However, Dworkin's distinction between personal and external preferences may not support all the conclusions that he reaches. For example, on the issue of free speech, even if external preferences for silencing other people's disagreeable expressions of opinion are ignored, freedom of speech may not be protected, since as Haworth

(1979, p.417) points out, a majority may have personal preferences that would justify its restriction. 'They may see, for example, that they are unlikely to want to criticise the government', and 'that to tolerate expression of minority dissent would detract from the effectiveness of policies from which they personally benefit'. The fact is that Dworkin's distinction between personal and external preferences only gives unequivocal endorsement to one freedom – the freedom not to have one's conduct determined by other people's external preferences. Beyond that, no particular liberty is protected, since in almost every case of freedom, personal preferences could clash (Jones, 1989a, pp.32–3).

Moreover, there are considerable difficulties in the way of applying the distinction between personal and external preferences. Dworkin himself admits that any attempt to separate personal from external preferences is 'impossible', and that consequently the distinction is 'in itself of limited practical significance'. This is so, Dworkin explains, for both institutional and psychological reasons; institutionally, no voting system can accurately discriminate between personal and external preferences, not least because, psychologically, many of a person's preferences contain elements of both personal and external preferences (Dworkin, [R.], 1978, p.276).

There is one final issue: even if Dworkin can overcome the above difficulties to demonstrate how the principle of equal concern and respect entails certain freedoms, as a justification of liberty this argument cannot be complete until he can show why the equality principle itself is a valuable one. That is to say, if liberty is derived from equality, then liberty is only valuable if equality is valuable. But Dworkin ([R.], 1978, pp.272–3) declines to justify his principle of equal concern and respect, apparently assuming that its value may be taken for granted: 'few citizens, and even fewer politicians, would now admit to political convictions that contradict the principle of equal concern and respect'. But the case for the principle of equal concern and respect must be argued, not assumed to be generally acceptable.

Conclusion on the argument of equality

Dworkin's attempt to derive a justification for certain freedoms from the principle of equal concern and respect is flawed. The principle is so elastic that it can be interpreted as justifying almost any liberty, or any restriction on liberty. Moreover no justification is offered for the principle itself. Nevertheless, despite these flaws, the Dworkinian notion that the principle of equal concern and respect serves as a means of distinguishing between justifiable and unjustifiable freedoms cannot be dismissed. His claim that the most important freedoms are those which are necessary in order to secure to persons the respect to which they are entitled as persons is intuitively appealing. The two difficulties with Dworkin's principle – that the principle can be applied to reach conflicting conclusions concerning which freedoms fall into which category (justifiable and unjustifiable), and that he offers no justification for the principle itself – may indicate that more work needs to be done in order to substantiate the intuition which we find so appealing, rather than that the intuition is unsound. In the next and final section, an attempt is made to justify freedom on grounds that it promotes utility – an argument that is more empirical in character than any of the preceding arguments, but as a result it is one that is more exposed to the charge of contingency.

6   The utility argument

Utility is the fourth of the explicitly moral justifications of liberty. Like the autonomy justification, the utility justification is, however, in danger of circularity, in that if liberty is interpreted as 'doing what one wants', then given the close connection between want-satisfaction and utility (utility is often regarded as synonymous with doing what one wants), the utility justification would amount to arguing that want-satisfaction (liberty) is a means to want-satisfaction (utility). To avoid this circularity, I will separate the discussion of the utilitarian justification into two parts; firstly to look at the utilitarian arguments for liberty conceived not as doing what one wants, but as a form of interpersonal freedom, particularly the absence of impediments and (more rarely) the availability of choices; secondly, to look at arguments for justifying the principle of utility itself as a form of freedom – that defined as doing what one wants. I begin with the first part.

The most sustained and influential attempt to justify interpersonal freedom on utilitarian grounds was made by Mill in his essay *On*

Liberty. Mill claims that freedom is a vital source of both individual well-being and social benefit. Freedom promotes individual well-being, because in matters of personal conduct each is a better judge of her own good than is society or the government (Mill, 1975, p.18). To this claim we might add the observation that the wider the range of options available to the agent, the greater the likelihood that she will satisfy her desires. Moreover, even if my existing range of options is sufficient to provide me with what I presently want, further options are still of value to me, because my preferences might change (Jones & Sugden, 1982, p.52). Furthermore, acts of choosing are in themselves important to well-being, irrespective of the choices made, in that they help to develop certain personality traits such as self-confidence, self-knowledge and strength of character, which are additional sources of value to the agent (Mill, 1975, pp.73,74,83).

This brings us to the social benefits that Mill believes are derived from interpersonal freedom. He argues (1975, p.87) that 'the only unfailing and permanent source of improvement is liberty'. In particular, Mill singles out freedom of thought and speech as prime catalysts of progress; people should be free to hold and express whatever opinions they like, not because their opinions are their own business, but because, on the contrary, they are a public benefaction. Mill denies that any opinion can be harmful, unless its manner of expression is inflammatory. Even the expression of a false belief is beneficial, since by challenging the true belief, it helps to prevent it degenerating from 'living truth' into 'dead dogma'. We need not fear that false beliefs will drive out true beliefs, since if they compete freely, true beliefs will in the end prevail (Bagehot, 1891, p.425). Schauer (1982, p.79) explains how freedom of speech may also serve as a catharsis or safety-valve for the peaceful expression of dissent, thereby reducing the likelihood of resort to acts of violence. It may also reinforce the sense of legitimation of government, since 'people may place greater trust in a government that is willing to hear and consider a wide range of arguments'. Having the opportunity to participate in public debate may make people 'more inclined to obey even those laws with which they disagree'. Moreover, the quality of governmental decisions is likely to improve by allowing prior public discussion of policy issues. Freedom of action also contributes to social happiness, in that experiments in living provide alternative models for people to choose between (Jones & Sugden, 1982, p.53).

A more unusual and dramatic utilitarian argument for interpersonal freedom is that a free society is one that is less likely than an unfree society to engage in warfare. Rummel (1983, p.29) has advanced this argument in terms of two propositions; (i) 'Libertarian systems mutually preclude violence (violence will occur between states only if at least one is nonlibertarian), (ii) 'Freedom inhibits violence (the more libertarian a state, the less it tends to be involved in violence)'. Rummel claims that evidence of all state conflicts since 1816 supports these propositions. Hence it may be argued that a very strong justification for freedom in society is that it reduces (or even eliminates) the risk of international violence.

Another unusual utilitarian argument for interpersonal freedom is that a free society promotes longer life expectancy. Frohock and Sylvan (1983, p.546) point out that there is a strong statistical correlation between freedom and the length of human life. According to the findings of Frohock and Sylvan, which were based on 1979 data, 59 per cent of the 54 countries classified as 'Not Free' enjoyed a life expectancy of only 49 years, whereas 57 per cent of the 44 countries classified as 'Free' enjoyed a life expectancy of 70 + years.

These utilitarian justifications for freedom have, however, been much criticised. The critics have challenged both the claim that freedom contributes to individual well-being, and the claim that freedom contributes to social benefit.

(a) Individual well-being

The claim that interpersonal freedom promotes individual happiness has been criticised on two counts. Firstly, individuals may not be the best judges of their own well-being. Most liberals, including Mill, endorse some restrictions which are designed to prevent a person for her own good from choosing to do something (for example, Mill forbade self-enslavement). English law forbids duelling, prize-fighting, consenting to one's own assault, and drug abuse, on the ground that we cannot assume that people engaging in such activities know their own interest best. Moreover, people sometimes make decisions in rash and ill-considered ways, or when their minds are disturbed (Hart, 1963, p.33), and they might be happier if prevented from choosing for themselves in such circumstances. (I myself would certainly be happier if tobacco were removed from the face of the earth!)

A defender of Mill might, however, reply to these points by arguing that although in principle A might be in some way a better judge of B's interest than is B herself, in practice if we try to run a society in which external judgements were generally enforced on people, the result would be less happiness, since there would be more bad paternalistic judgements than good paternalistic judgements. Hence, in policy terms, it is better to run a society as if each person were the best judge of her own interest, even though that might not always be true. Moreover, why should we accept that the paternalism which exists in English law is justified?

The second criticism of the claim that interpersonal freedom promotes happiness is that even when individuals are the best judge of their own well being, increased freedom may not always enhance that well-being. Jones and Sugden (1982, p.52) point out, for example, that if a person wants only option X, then his freedom to choose Y or Z rather than X, adds nothing to his utility. Of course, the utilitarian will reply that while at the present moment he may only want option X, he may in the future change his preferences, and therefore he has an interest in ensuring that his choices are as numerous as possible. Moreover, there is utility in the actual act of rejecting options, in so far as all choice is an act of self-affirmation.

However, to set against these advantages there is often disutility in increased choice. For example, an additional option may expose an agent to social influences which pressurise her into doing something that she does not want to do. Suppose people are allowed to bequeath property on their death; a wealthholder who would prefer to spend all her property on herself may be worse off than if she were forbidden to leave anything to her heirs, since she may be exposed to unwelcome pressure or attention from hopeful heirs (Dworkin, [G.], 1982, p.52). Increased choice may also entail substantial information costs to the chooser, in terms of the additional time and energy required to acquire information and make decisions (Kelman, 1981, p.228). These costs may be so great as to lead to 'information-overload', leaving the agent worse off than with less choice (Davis, [M.], 1978/9, p.169). Psychic costs may also rise, since as a result of newly-available options, people may worry more about whether they have made the right decision. A telling example of the painful burden of increased responsibility is that which has now been placed upon expectant parents by the development of the medical technique of amniocentesis together with new legislation widening the grounds for abortion (Dworkin, [G.], 1982, p.51). Another cost that may be involved in the addition of an option arises where that option is made available to everyone else at the same time, thereby undermining its utility to any particular individual. For example, if the price of my having a car is that everyone else has a car, with the consequent damage to the environment in which I live, then I may prefer that cars had never been invented (Hart, 1975, p.248).

Given these costs of freedom, it may well be rational for people in some circumstances to renounce their freedom for the sake of their happiness (Kelman, 1981, p.242). According to some psychiatrists, freedom is sometimes a source of anguish rather than happiness, and individuals may experience more pleasure than pain by giving up certain choices. For example, 'by foreclosing in advance the idea of alternative sexual relationships (foreclosing not by declining options but by abandoning the very idea of an option) one can express to one's partner the special character of one's relationship' (Dworkin, [G.], 1982, p.57). Similarly, the religious vows of poverty, chastity and obedience which are taken by priests, nuns and monks represent a renunciation of freedom in exchange for spiritual contentment (although, of course, their *motive* for taking these vows may well be to register spiritual conviction rather than to obtain spiritual contentment). Even a condition of voluntary slavery could be justified on utilitarian grounds.

However, the significance of many of these arguments should not be exaggerated. While it may be true that there are circumstances in which increased choice results in decreased utility for an agent, it may be equally true that there are many more circumstances in which lack of choice results in decreased utility for most people.

(b) Social benefit

The utilitarian claim that freedom of speech promotes social benefit has been much criticised. The critics deny that truth depends upon freedom of discussion, pointing out that we accept most of the truths of science and morality quite readily without opposed false views being pressed upon us (Stephen, 1967, p.76). We need not, for example, be assailed by flat-earthers or by paedophiles to know with conviction that the earth is round or that having sex with children is wrong. Indeed, on the contrary, the risk is that instead of vivifying and reinforcing our true beliefs, being bombarded by false opinions might very well weaken our hold on the truth (McCloskey, 1968, p.334). As Schauer (1982, pp.75,27) points out, 'unfortunately falsity is often to many people more appealing than truth, especially when accepting falsity requires less effort than identifying truth'. Truth has no inherent tendency to triumph over error in a free and equal encounter between them.

Even if free discussion does lead to truth, truth is not synonymous with social utility. There are circumstances in which the damage that free speech can inflict upon social utility outweighs any benefit it may yield by promoting truth. Mill himself (1975, p.69) recognises this, in accepting the necessity for restraints upon inflammatory speeches where danger to life and property could result – as in the case of an angry mob outside a corndealer's house. This recognition weakens the claim that free speech necessarily serves as a safety valve by defusing the violence of opposition to government policy (Schauer, 1982, p. 80). To these criticisms, however, the utilitarian might reasonably reply that all they demonstrate is that utilitarians cannot satisfactorily maintain that free speech *per se*, in all of its manifestations, promotes social happiness, but such a demonstration does not fundamentally undermine the utilitarian justification of interpersonal freedom; it merely qualifies it in certain respects. It leaves intact the more modest and realistic claim by utilitarians that *for the most part* free speech promotes truth, and *for the most part* truth in turn promotes social utility.

The utilitarian claim that freedom of *action* promotes social utility is even more vehemently contested than is the claim that freedom of *speech* does so (Bagehot, 1891, pp.435–6). Mill himself does not argue that *all* actions should be free from interference; on the contrary, he readily accepts that many acts must be forbidden because of their damaging effects on the happiness of others. Hence, for example, any act which violates rights, such as assault or fraud, cannot be tolerated, since the disutility to the victim outweighs any pleasure to the perpetrator. But Mill does insist that where an act does not affect or harm other people's rights – a self-regarding action – it ought to be immune from interference.

However, this immunity of so-called self-regarding actions has been challenged by Mill's critics. Devlin, for instance, argues that no hard and fast line can be drawn between the private and the public spheres of conduct, since almost every kind of 'private' behaviour will have some public effects. In the very nature of things, vice cannot be private; 'private' vice is actually public canker. 'A nation of debauchees would not in 1940 have responded satisfactorily to Winston Churchill's call to blood and toil and sweat and tears' (Devlin, 1965, p.111). Devlin (1965, p.17) also argues that Mill is wrong to sweep aside the feelings of outraged sensibility suffered by other people when contemplating a person's private immorality. If the genuine feeling of society at large is that a particular private vice is 'so abominable that its mere presence is an offence', then, says Devlin, 'I do not see how society can be denied the right to eradicate it'. On utilitarian grounds, then, the suffering of outraged people must be taken into account.

Devlin may well be exaggerating the damage that private vice inflicts upon society, but his argument does draw attention to a central difficulty faced by any utilitarian justification of freedom – that on a utilitarian calculation, the pleasure taken by an intolerant majority in persecuting a minority might outweigh the pain suffered by the victimised minority (Ten, 1980, p.34). There is such a thing as the pleasure of malevolence, as Bentham pointed out, and in certain cases it is conceivable that the pleasure gained by a majority in punishing the self-regarding actions of a despised minority (say homosexuals), would exceed the pain suffered by those punished. If external preferences are taken into account, utilitarianism is consistent with illiberalism (Dworkin, [R.], 1978, p.236). Dworkin argues that the only way liberalism can be rescued from this difficulty is by ignoring external preferences in the utilitarian calculations. But even if this is a practicable means of rescuing liberalism, it raises a serious question for utilitarianism: what utilitarian reason can there be for ignoring external preferences? Are we to say that the pleasure or pain that we experience in contemplating what other people do, is not genuine pleasure or pain, or is not legitimate pleasure or pain, or is pleasure or pain that is inferior in value to the pleasure or pain we take in what we ourselves do? Any of these interpretations is open to the charge of arbitrariness and threatens the coherence and credibility of the utilitarian calculus.

Rummel's claim, that interpersonal freedom reduces the risk of warfare – in that libertarian states *never* aggress on one another, and that the more libertarian a state, the less it tends to be involved in violence – has been challenged by Vincent. Vincent (1987) argues that Rummel's claim is founded upon inadequate statistical data, arising out of controversial definitions of freedom and violence, and that use of more adequate data yields no support for Rummel's findings. The claim rehearsed by Frohock and Sylvan that in free societies citizens live longer, may be countered by the argument that a strong statistical correlation between liberty and long life expectancy does not in itself demonstrate any causal connection between freedom and longevity, since a third factor (say a plenitude of natural resources) may be the cause of both freedom and longevity.

It seems, then, that the attempt to justify liberty as a means to the promotion of social benefit faces considerable difficulties, though once again these difficulties may be exaggerated. While there are circumstances in which interpersonal freedom fails to promote social benefit, there may be many more circumstances in which it succeeds in doing so. Let us now turn to the second part of the utility justification of liberty – namely the argument, not that liberty conceived in interpersonal terms is a means to utility, but that utility is itself a form of liberty, conceived in intrapersonal terms of doing what one wants, and as such, is a valuable human good. This raises the question 'what is valuable about doing what one wants?' or, on the not unreasonable assumption that doing what one wants makes one happy, 'what is valuable about utility?'. The answer given by utilitarians such as Mill is that while we cannot *prove* utility to be valuable, we can point out that since (it seems) everyone desires to be happy rather than miserable, that fact *suggests* that happiness is desirable. We can also point out that a tolerable case can be made out for saying that the basic moral rules in society – rules of justice, for example – have been fashioned and sanctified not because of their intrinsic rectitude, but because of their enormous utility, enabling more people to do what they want more of the time.

However, even if happiness (either individual or collective) is universally desired, not everything that is universally desired is valuable. There are many things, for example, which I desire to do, that I recognise it would be quite wrong for me to do. Moreover, while it may be true that moral rules such as the rules of virtue and justice promote utility, their moral status may rest upon an independent basis of right, and in some cases they may demand conduct that appears to be contrary to the principle of utility.

Conclusion on the argument of utility

The discussion of the view that interpersonal freedom is a means to utility indicates that although it may well be true that liberty is an important promoter of both individual and social well-being, it is by no means clear that either freedom in general or any particular liberty can be unequivocally justified on a utilitarian basis. Moreover, the utilitarian justification of interpersonal freedom is particularly vulnerable to the charge of contingency (Flathman, 1987, p.230). If, for example, the popular mood or national character were to change, then liberties which were previously secure – because they maximised happiness – could be undermined – because they no longer maximised happiness. This is an unreliable justification for freedom. Nevertheless, it would be misleading to conclude that the difficulties we have discussed render futile the instrumentalist utilitarian justification for interpersonal freedom. What the discussion has shown is that we cannot take for granted the claim that interpersonal freedoms always promote utility; the onus lies on the utilitarian to produce the evidence which is necessary to identify the circumstances in which they do so.

The discussion of the view that utility embodies a conception of freedom – the intrapersonal conception of doing what one wants – indicates that to justify freedom on this basis requires a justification of the principle of utility itself. But since not all actions in which people do what they want are morally defensible, such a justification must remain at best conditional.

Conclusion on the justifications of freedom

Three conclusions emerge from the discussions in this chapter. The first conclusion is that it is not convincing to attempt to justify freedom *simpliciter*. None of the arguments considered can successfully demonstrate that freedom *per se* is unconditionally a good thing. Indeed, strictly interpreted, none of them seriously attempts such an implausible task. The arguments of presumption and rights serve as formats for justificatory arguments, rather than as justificatory arguments in themselves. The arguments of neutrality, autonomy, equality and utility serve as principles or rules by which to distinguish between justifiable and unjustifiable liberties. In this sense, Berlin is right to claim that liberty *in itself*, like all other ultimate values, cannot be 'proved', but must be regarded as a basic axiom, a starting point, which is either assumed or denied as part of one's moral value system. Arguments must presuppose some first principle which itself cannot be demonstrated; perhaps liberty in general is just such a first principle. 'For the man devoted to liberty, there is nothing which *makes* liberty important. And he has no reason for his devotion.' (Rhees, 1969, p.84).

The second conclusion is that while freedom *per se* cannot be satisfactorily justified, nevertheless particular liberties may be defended by reference to one or other (or more than one) of the six justifications considered above. For example, the argument of presumption, drawing as it does some of its rationale from the jurisprudential axiom of innocence until guilt is proven, might help to prepare the format of a case for certain legal liberties such as Habeas Corpus. The argument of neutrality, appealing as it does to the precept that no conception of the good can be shown to be superior to any other, could add some weight to the demand for religious toleration. The argument of rights, with its presupposition that all moral agents are bearers of rights, could help in the formulation of a claim that enslavement is wrong. The argument of autonomy, connected as it is to the principle of self-determination, might be employed in aid of opposition to insidious forms of commercial promotion. The argument of equality, requiring that people be treated with respect, could be used to help in the protection of the disabled and the hospitalised. Finally, the argument of utility, tied to the notion of the public interest, could reinforce the demand for freedom of scientific research. Moreover, it is possible to value liberties for more than one reason; for example, religious freedom could be supported by arguments drawn not only from the principle of neutrality, but also from the principles of rights, autonomy, equality and utility. Hence, despite the difficulties we have found in the way of justifying freedom in general, support may be available from one or more of the six justificatory arguments for certain particular liberties.

The third conclusion is that, while there is some natural affinity between the autonomy justificatory argument and the self-determination conception of freedom, and between the utility justificatory argument and the doing what one wants conception of freedom, there is no mode of justification that is necessarily restricted to any particular conception of freedom, nor does any particular conception of freedom require a mode of justification exclusive to itself. In the main, perhaps surprisingly, most justificatory arguments apply to most conceptions of freedom. For example, even the most idiosyncratic conception of freedom – that of self-mastery – can be supported on grounds of right, autonomy and utility; while even the most specific justificatory argument – that of autonomy – can be employed to justify freedom conceived as availability of choices, status, self-determination and doing what one wants.

4 Measurement of Freedom

Whenever freedom is discussed we customarily take for granted not only its meaning and its value, but also its comparative nature. In doing so, however, we may overlook the fact that any attempt made to compare and contrast the extent of freedom enjoyed by different individuals or different countries, or by the same individuals or countries at different times, faces considerable conceptual and practical difficulties. What these difficulties are, and whether they can be overcome, are the central issues of this chapter. But first a note about the conceptions of freedom to be used in this chapter. Most attention will be focused upon the interpersonal conceptions of freedom – i.e. absence of impediments, availability of choices, effective power and status. The reason for this is that it is in relation to these conceptions of freedom that the central issues of measurement generally arise. For instance, if we are trying to compare the extent of freedom in the USSR with that in the USA, we are more likely to be interested in the legal and social impediments which exist respectively in these countries, than in the extent to which Russians and Americans manifest the quality of self-mastery. Indeed, it has been suggested that the very notion of measuring freedom presupposes an interpersonal conception of freedom, since intrapersonal conceptions of freedom are not susceptible to precise, i.e. quantitative, measurement. Some critics have argued, however, that quantitative measurement misses the wood for the trees: what we may be able to *measure* (i.e. what is quantitatively precise), may not be what is *important* about freedom, and so any comparative conclusion reached on a quantitative basis would not tell us much of significance about the respective extents of freedom in, for example, the USSR and the USA. According to this argument, therefore, what we must do is to make qualitative *judgements*, not attempt quantitative *measurements*, in order to compare the extent of freedom in different countries.

There are two distinct issues here; first, whether comparisons of extents of freedom should be quantitative measurements or qualitative judgements; second whether we ought to ignore intrapersonal conceptions of freedom in making such comparisons. These are separate issues, since 'interpersonal' is not synonymous with 'quantitative'; and 'intrapersonal' is not synonymous with 'qualitative'. In this chapter I will discuss at length the issue of quantitative versus qualitative modes of comparison, and although I will concentrate most attention upon the interpersonal conceptions of freedom, one or other of the intrapersonal conceptions will periodically come into focus – in particular, that of self-determination, which is discussed as one of the five major issues raised in the measurement debate.

Many critics argue that it is inherently impossible to measure freedom. A statement typical of the view of such critics is the following;

> 'liberty is not a commodity to be weighed and measured. I am free to do x, y, and z, but not p, q, and r – but there is no substance called 'freedom' of which I can therefore possess more or less, according to the particular combination of things permissible and things forbidden. All that can be said is that I am free in some ways and not in others; that some are more important than others; and that the condition of being free in some ways is that I should not be free in others. But there is no way of casting a resultant sum of freedom.' (Benn and Peters, 1959, pp.214–15)

Ryan ([A.], 1975, p.359) accepts the implication that this rules out precise international comparisons: 'there is no simple calculus of liberty. We cannot add up gains to freedom and subtract losses to freedom, in order to rank societies on a libertarian scale like gross national product per head'. Amnesty International refuses to produce a comparative assessment of countries' violations of human rights – i.e. an international league table of unfreedom – partly because of lack of reliable information, but mainly because of what it claims is the inherent impossibility of comparing unlike situations.

However, other bodies are less inhibited. Freedom House, for example, publishes an annual review of the extent of freedom in the world, rating every country on a scale of one to seven for its level of liberty in each of two spheres – political and civil freedom – and producing an overall classification for every country into one of three categories:-

Free – where the combined grade for political and civil freedom is 1 or 2

Partly Free – where the combined grade for political and civil freedom is 3 or 4 or 5

Not Free – where the combined grade for political and civil freedom is 6 or 7.

For the year 1986, 56 countries were classified as 'free'; 57 countries 'partly free'; and 53 countries 'not free'. During the period 1973–86, Gastil (1987), the author of the reviews, claimed that the extent of freedom had increased in 67 states, decreased in 58 states, and remained unchanged in 42 states.

The Freedom House findings have apparently been influential in forming American foreign policy attitudes towards certain states, despite considerable academic criticism. The main criticism is that the ratings given to countries are impressionistic rather than quantitatively precise, reflecting the ideologically-loaded views of Freedom House. One critic complained that 'the Freedom House scoring scale is hardly better than a simple division into "good" and "bad" countries'. (Banks, 1986, p.659; cf. Schoultz, 1980, p.95). Gastil has admitted that his method of arriving at the ratings is not rigorously quantitative, but he has defended it by asserting that a purely quantitative method would omit important qualitative factors. He refers to Dahl's experience of using a purely quantitative method: 'Dahl used such a scheme in developing his list of democracies. Yet he notes that in at least one case he had to adjust the results to obtain the relationships that he intuitively "knew" were correct in spite of the quantitative apparatus' (Gastil, 1987, p.85). An unkind critic might conclude from this that Gastil chose to avoid precise quantitative measurements because he feared that the results would undermine his personal, intuitive, qualitative judgements about the extent of freedom that exists in some states.

A more rigorously quantitative attempt to measure and compare the extent of freedom in the nations of the world – or rather 90 of them (countries with a population of less than 1 million were omitted, and the data concerning 30 further countries was insufficient to allow an assessment) – has been made by Humana in his *World Human Rights Guide* (1986). Questionnaire results in respect of each of 40 liberties were graded into the following four categories:

unqualified respect for the liberty or right – 3 points
occasional breach of the liberty or right – 2 points
frequent violation of the liberty or right – 1 point
constant pattern of violation of the liberty or right – 0 points

Humana set out to do explicitly and systematically what Gastil had done implicitly and impressionistically – to take account of the fact that some liberties are more significant than others. Humana weighted seven out of the 40 liberties by a factor of three. The liberties he chose to so weight were the physical freedoms – e.g. freedom from forced labour, detention without charge, torture, corporal and capital punishment. Accordingly, the maximum possible points score for the 40 questions, after weighting, but before conversion to a percentage, was $162 - $ i.e. $(33 \times 3) + (7 \times 3 \times 3)$. For example, Egypt was given a rating of 59 per cent: this was based on 57 points from the 33 un-weighted questions, plus 39 points from the seven weighted questions – $(57 + 39) \times 100/162 = 59$ per cent. Humana (1986, pp.3–4) was fully aware of the controversial nature of his somewhat subjective mode of weighting liberties, but defended it on grounds that, for example, a person who is being tortured or locked up indefinitely in an unlit cell, is suffering a greater degree of deprivation than a person who is denied a vote or uncensored newspapers.

From our point of view, the central question raised by Humana's weighting scheme is this: do the seven physical liberties embody a greater amount of freedom than the remaining 33 non-physical liberties, or do they constitute more valuable liberties? In other words, is the weighting process quantitative or qualitative? Moreover, why is it only these seven freedoms that are to be weighted? Why are they all given the same weighting? And why is that weighting factor three? It is worth noting that, according to Banks, there is a high degree of correlation between the findings of Gastil and Humana (Banks, 1986, p.655).

Let us begin our discussion of questions such as these by referring to the views of Berlin (1969, p.130f) on the subject of assessing the extent of freedom.

'The extent of my freedom seems to depend on (a) how many possibilities are open to me...; (b) how easy or difficult each of these possibilities is to actualise; (c) how important in my plan of life...these possibilities are...; (d) how far they are closed and opened by deliberate human acts; (e) what value...the general sentiment of the society...puts on the various possibilities.'

This statement of five scales of freedom is a useful starting point for a rehearsal of the problems facing any attempt to measure liberty. Berlin himself, while acknowledging that severe difficulties stand in the way of such an exercise – 'It may well be that there are many incommensurable kinds and degrees of freedom, and that they cannot be drawn up on any single scale of magnitude' – claims that 'provided we do not demand precise measurement, we can give valid reasons for saying that the average subject of the King of Sweden is, on the whole, a good deal freer today than the average citizen of...Albania'.

It is this sort of claim that I wish to test by discussing five major issues: 1. the delimitation of actions; 2. the commensurability of actions; 3. the differential importance of actions; 4. the degree of difficulty of performing actions; 5. the determinism of actions.

1 The delimitation of actions

At first sight, Berlin's scale (a) – counting up the possibilities open to an agent – seems a perfectly sensible and practicable mode of measuring the extent of that agent's freedom, based as it is on the widely supported conception of freedom in terms of the availability of choices. However, there are difficulties entailed by such a computation. Steiner (1983, p.74) raises the objection that it ignores the extent of prevented options. Simply computing the acts that A is free to do is an inadequate mode of assessing the extent of A's freedom; we must know not only what A is free to do, but also what A is not free to do, before we can properly measure the extent of A's freedom, still less compare it with that of B. Accordingly, Steiner suggests a formula to measure freedom which takes account of both the free and the unfree acts of A and B. The formula is $Fr/Fr + Ur$, where Fr is the total number of one's free actions, and Ur is the total number of one's unfree actions. In effect, this is to add to the dimension of liberty interpreted by Berlin in terms of the availability of choices, the dimension of liberty interpreted by Gastil and Humana in terms of the absence of impediments. Steiner's formula sets out in the form of a fraction the extent of a person's freedom: the greater the number of her free acts proportionate to her unfree acts, the larger the size of the fraction, and so the more extensive her freedom.

Steiner may, however, be criticised for insisting that we need to compute unfree acts separately from free acts. If we have a computation of what acts people *can* do (their free acts), this in itself tells us what they *cannot* do (their unfree acts) – they cannot do anything other than the things that they can do. Conversely, if we have a computation of what people *cannot* do (their unfree acts), that in itself tells us what they *can* do (their free acts) – they can do anything other than the things they cannot do. This is a criticism that we have noted in Chapter 2, in relation to both the absence of impediments and availability of choices conceptions of freedom. In the latter discussion it was observed, however, that options are not *always* the converse of impediments. Robinson Crusoe did not have the option of going to the theatre, yet no one impeded him from doing so. Only if we define impediments in such a way that they must exist wherever there is a lack of choice, can we treat impediments and choices as mutually implied by each other. For example, in the case of Robinson Crusoe, we could claim that the non-option of going to the theatre was an implication of his being shipwrecked (a natural impediment), or was entailed by the refusal of maritime nations to launch a rescue attempt on his behalf (human impediment). But these are somewhat contrived manipulations of the notion of an impediment; a more reasonable view of the issue is to acknowledge that impediments and choices are not always opposite sides of the same coin, since each may exist independently of the other, and to accept Steiner's claim that we need to measure the extent of both freedoms (choices) and unfreedoms (impediments).

Whatever basis we choose for our computation, we must be able to determine what acts a person is free and/or unfree to do. But how can we identify all of a person's free and/or unfree acts? How can we know that we have included all the possible options open and closed to someone? Drawing attention to this problem – 'the actions which a person is free or unfree to do may be infinitely numerous' – Steiner (1983, p.74) sweeps it aside, however, on grounds that it is only incumbent upon us to include in our calculations those acts of which we can and do have knowledge. Not unreasonably, then, the onus is placed upon the critic to point out which free and/or unfree actions the measurer of freedom has failed to include in the calculations.

A more serious problem posed by the attempt to aggregate freedoms and unfreedoms is the difficulty of determining precisely what is to count as a single action or option. Many actions are not discrete entities. For example, the action of voting has a large number of component parts: travelling to the polling station; identifying oneself to the officials; taking a ballot paper to a booth; reading its contents; deliberating on the choice to be made; inserting a cross next to a name; dropping the slip into a ballot-box; travelling back home. Do we count each of these component actions separately, or do we count the entire activity of voting as a single act? The fact is that virtually every action can be broken down into component actions, and this process of sub-division can go on almost indefinitely; the point at which we should call a halt to it seems entirely arbitrary. To avoid this problem of indefinite individuation, we might consider the possibility of finding a basic unit of measurement of human body movements. If all our acts could be reduced to their basic physical (i.e. spatio-temporal) body movements, then there would be a clear limit to the extent of individuation. In the example of voting, each component action which 'could have occurred even if the others had not' (Steiner, 1983, p.76) would therefore be counted as a single act.

However, the question then becomes – how do we know what amount of freedom each such single act embodies? This raises questions of commensurability and importance, to which we turn in the next two sections. But before doing so, there is a further issue of delimitation to be considered. We face the choice of counting either *act-types*, or a person's *actual actions*. An 'act-type' denotes a general category of action, such as the freedom to visit a foreign country. An 'actual action' denotes a specific kind of action, such as the freedom to visit a particular part of a foreign country for a given period of time. Whichever choice we make presents difficulties. For instance, if we count *act-types*, we will underestimate the extent of freedom in certain cases.

'If I can only go to East Berlin for one day, but you can go for a year, it will not do to say that we are equally free to "go to East Berlin". And if I can only go to East Berlin but you can go anywhere in East Germany, it will not do simply to say that we can both "go to East Germany". The spatio-temporal parts of actions must be specified if we are to show how much more free one individual is than another.' (Carter, 1988, p.7)

But if we count people's *actual actions*, are we not in danger of judging that a larger country is freer than a smaller country simply because it contains within it more people, and therefore more actual actions? Hence, the selection of either alternative, act-types or actual actions, could create anomalies. (I return to this issue in Chapter 5.)

2 The commensurability of actions

Even if we can satisfactorily individuate all actions into their irreducible discrete bodily movements, we have somehow to judge how these bodily movements compare in terms of freedom. The difficulty is that there appears to be no basic common unit of measurement of human body movements which we can use as a yardstick to calculate the amount of liberty in irreducible single acts. Steiner (1983, pp.82–3) assumes that each irreducible single act is equivalent in its amount of freedom; i.e. that if we can reduce actions to their irreducible component acts, then we do not need to look for the amount of freedom within these irreducible acts; we simply take these acts and ask whether people are free/unfree to perform them. But irreducible component acts may contain within them differential amounts of freedom. Carter has suggested to me a striking analogy to make this point; when a greengrocer sells apples, if they are of comparable size, she may well not bother to weigh them, but sell them for a certain sum per apple; if, however, the apples vary in size, she will weigh them, and sell them at so much per pound. What Steiner seems to assume is that irreducible acts are like apples of the same size, whereas the truth may be that they are like apples of different sizes, and that they must be weighed rather than counted, if reliable comparisons are to be made about the extent of freedom within them. The trouble is, of course, that we are not able to weigh freedoms in the way that a greengrocer is able to weigh apples.

There are two distinct difficulties involved in attempting to count actions: one is quantitative and the other is qualitative. The quantitative difficulty is the one that we have been concerned with so far – namely the awkwardness of reducing different kinds of bodily movements to a single scale. To give another example to illustrate the quantitative difficulty; if we compare freedom of speech with freedom to walk in the park, how much movement of the larynx is equivalent to how much movement of the feet? The qualitative difficulty lies in the fact that freedoms differ in kind as well as in extent. To reduce freedom of speech to a series of movements of the larynx, and to reduce freedom to walk in the park to a series of movements of the feet, and to compare these two series of movements quantitatively, seems to caricature both types of freedom. Steiner has pointed out to me in private correspondence, however, that this criticism is to confuse acts with the freedom to perform acts. 'It's not "*freedom* of speech" that's being reduced to a series of larynx movements, but rather, speech itself', and this is just how physicists would attempt to measure motion. Nevertheless, it does seem that a problem of qualitative incommensurability remains. We cannot evaluate *freedom* of speech in a way which ignores the fact that it is freedom of *speech*.

Do these problems of commensurability mean that we cannot make any meaningful comparisons of freedom? Not necessarily; we may be able to sidestep the problems of both quantitative and qualitative commensurability by conducting Paretian comparisons. That is to say, we may conclude that a citizen in country X has more freedom than a citizen in country Y if she can do everything that citizen Y can do, plus one or more additional action(s) (Feinberg, 1980, p.10; Crocker, 1980, p.54; Taylor, [M.], 1982, p.151). Oppenheim uses the notion of Paretian superiority to affirm that

'Hitler had more total freedom than Adenauer. Hitler was to a great extent free to act as he pleased with respect to his cabinet, party, army, and larger population; under the present constitutional regime, the chancellor's freedom is limited by the other branches of the government and by the electorate. Consequently, both the domain and the scope of Hitler's freedom was greater.' (Oppenheim, 1961, p.201)

However, situations of Paretian superiority are rare. In most cases of comparison, no situation is unambiguously Pareto-superior to another. Moreover, some situations which appear to be Paretian, may turn out, on closer inspection, to be non-Paretian. This is the case, for example, with Oppenheim's comparison of the respective freedoms of Hitler and Adenauer. Although it may very well be true that Hitler possessed many more freedoms than did Adenauer, in that he was subject to far fewer constitutional restrictions, nevertheless there are some respects in which Adenauer was freer than Hitler. For instance, Adenauer could travel more freely abroad than could Hitler, since Hitler was *persona non grata* in many more foreign countries. We could only conclude that Hitler was freer than Adenauer, either by assuming, like Steiner, that all freedoms are in principle quantitatively commensurate, and that the more numerous freedoms possessed by Hitler, but denied to Adenauer, quantitatively outweighed the fewer freedoms possessed by Adenauer, but denied to Hitler; or by asserting that the freedoms enjoyed by Hitler were qualitatively superior to those enjoyed by Adenauer. We have discussed the problems of quantitative commensurability, but we have only touched on the difficulties of qualitative commensurability. Let us now examine these difficulties in some detail, by investigating Berlin's scale (c) concerning the differential importance of actions.

3 The importance of actions

A solution to the problem of qualitative incommensurability might be to assert that all freedoms can be ranked on a scale of importance, and that the higher up the scale, the greater the amount of significant freedom (Oppenheim, 1961, p.202). It is frequently claimed that measurement of freedom *must* take into account the fact that some actions are more important than others (or the converse fact that some impediments to freedom are more important than others). Unless this fact is recognised, it is argued, counter-intuitive conclusions will result. For instance, if the dimension of importance is ignored, traffic restrictions would be interpreted as a greater infringement of individual freedom than would restrictions on freedom of worship, since they impose more physical impediments on movement.

'We recognize that religion has been abolished in Albania, whereas it hasn't been in Britain. But on the other hand there are probably far fewer traffic lights per head in Tirana than in London... Suppose an apologist for Albanian Socialism were nevertheless to claim that this country was freer than Britain, because the number of acts restricted was far smaller. After all, only a minority of Londoners practise some religion in public places, but all have to negotiate their way through traffic. Those who do practice a religion generally do so on one day of the week, while they are held up at traffic lights every day. In sheer quantitative terms, the number of acts restricted by traffic lights must be greater than that restricted by a ban on public religious practice.' (Taylor, [C.], 1979, p.183)

This is, says Taylor, a 'diabolical defence of Albania as a free country'. Such counter-intuitive conclusions can only be avoided by recognising that some freedoms are more important than others. We will return to Taylor's argument in a moment, but first we must distinguish between the extrinsic and the intrinsic importance of actions. The extrinsic importance of an action refers to the significance of its consequences: the intrinsic importance of an action refers to the significance of the action itself. Beginning with *extrinsic importance*; if actions are to be counted purely in terms of their own basic bodily movements, then no account is thereby taken of the consequences or results of such actions. Hence, for example, two acts of moving my little finger would be counted equally, even though the first resulted in no further consequences (other than loosening up my metacarpal muscles), whereas the second resulted also in my successfully attracting the attention of the auctioneer. Surely, it has been argued, the latter act manifests more freedom than does the former act? The point being made here is that ineffective bodily movements yield less freedom than effective bodily movements. This is to add to the two conceptions of freedom already incorporated into the discussion – availability of choice and absence of impediments – a third conception, that of effective power.

However, any attempt to take consequences into account bristles with difficulty. For one thing, we do not always know what the consequences of an action are, especially the long-term consequences. For another thing, we could face once more the problem of an indefinite number of possible instances. As Carter has remarked to me in private correspondence; 'the problem here is no longer one of infinite division, but of infinite addition'. At what point do we stop listing consequences? It seems arbitrary to make assessments of freedom depend upon how many consequences we happen to list. Moreover, presumably we will have to find some way of discriminating between trivial consequences, which we would not want to enter into the calculations, and important consequences, which we would want to enter into the calculations, since the whole point of taking consequences into account is to distinguish important from unimportant actions. But attempts to discriminate between trivial and important consequences raise serious difficulties (see below).

One extrinsic factor of particular significance for the measurement of liberty is the effect of one freedom upon another freedom. Liberties may facilitate, or block, other liberties (Deutsch, 1962, pp.302–3). Feinberg (1980, p.37) describes this as the 'fecundity' dimension of liberty. However, the difficulty of measuring fecundity is considerable. How can we practicably estimate the net fruitfulness of one liberty in promoting other liberties? While it may be true that the fecundity (or infecundity) of some freedoms (such as committing suicide) is easy to calculate, in the case of other freedoms (such as educational opportunity) fecundity may be almost impossible to measure with any confidence, because of the unpredictability of the consequences for any particular agent.

Turning now to the *intrinsic importance* of actions, many writers follow Oppenheim's view that the extent of someone's freedom depends in part upon the intrinsic importance of the options open to them. Oppenheim (1961, p.207) claims that familiar sorts of comparisons are founded upon assessments of the significance of the freedoms compared: 'If we believe that there is greater liberty in the United States than in Soviet Russia, it is not, for example, because United States citizens are subject to fewer regulations than Soviet citizens, but because we are free in those respects which we value most'.

There are two questions raised by the attempt to measure the intrinsic importance of actions. The first question concerns the proper place of the notion of importance in a discussion of freedom. Many critics have argued that importance is an indicator of the value of freedom, not of its extent. Hence whatever importance is attached to an action, they claim, is irrelevant to the measurement of a person's freedom to perform that action. However, Jones has suggested to me that since the reason why we want to measure freedom is because we regard freedom as valuable (as important to people), if we can measure that value (that importance), then the question of how much freedom *qua* freedom (i.e. freedom independently of its value or importance) people have is a matter of comparatively little significance. Why should it matter whether you have 'more' freedom (in some quantitative, value-free sense) than me, if we are both agreed that the freedom that I have is more valuable than the freedom that you have? But isn't this just the critics' point – that we are not agreed on the relative importance of freedoms, and therefore if we are to compare states of freedom at all, we must discount value-laden elements in our view of it?

The second question raised by attempts to measure the intrinsic importance of actions is the practical one of how to calculate intrinsic importance. Some writers, such as Arneson, Loevinsohn and Draughon, imply that this calculation entails taking into account people's preferences. Loevinsohn (1976/7, p.233), for example, writes that the more important an action is to someone, the more he desires to do it, and the greater the loss of liberty if he is prevented from doing it. But is the importance of an action properly gauged by people's preferences? Taylor ([C.], 1979, p.184) rightly draws a distinction between what people want and what is important: 'it is a matter of the most banal experience that the purposes we know to be more significant are not always those which we desire with the greatest urgency to encompass'. Many evaluations of freedom are what Barry would call 'ideal-regarding', rather than 'want-regarding'. Hence when writers such as Taylor value freedom of worship more than free traffic flow, they are making that assessment on the basis of what they believe really ought to matter to human beings, rather than on the basis of what immediately concerns them in terms of their own wants. However, using preferences rather than judgements as the criterion of importance would make the task of calculating the importance of freedoms easier, since wants are empirically more identifiable, more common to different people, and more quantifiable, than are ideals.

Whether we use preferences or judgements to indicate the relative importance of freedoms, whose preferences/judgements do we use? Do we choose the preferences/judgements of the individual agent (Berlin's scale (c), the personal criterion), or the preferences/ judgements of the society in which the individual lives (Berlin's scale (e), the social criterion)? Writers who adopt the personal criterion are faced with the difficulty of determining whether A is freer than B, in the sense of having the more important freedoms, where A has one set of values by which she evaluates the importance of the options open and closed to her, and B has a different set of values by which he evaluates the importance of the same options open and closed to him. Writers who adopt the social criterion face the problem of selecting a ranked set of values for determining degrees of importance which is generally shared by members of the society.

Megone believes that we can avoid these difficulties by interpreting degrees of importance of actions in terms of their quantity of freedom. In other words, Megone is saying that we can reduce qualitative distinctions to a quantitative basis. Commenting on Taylor's example of the comparison between Albania and Britain, Megone (1987, pp.618–19) argues that 'If religious belief, of which the forms of worship are an important part, affects one's whole way of life, then a restraint on that affects a far higher quantity of activity than the imposition of a traffic light. This latter simply affects the speed at which citizens can travel along a certain route each day'. However, Taylor's point was that even if religious belief only affected the way of life of a small number of people – and therefore on Megone's quantitative scale, *could not* be of great significance (Megone's attempt to show that atheists have an interest in religious liberty is unconvincing) – freedom of worship was of much greater intrinsic human value than free traffic flow. This qualitative dimension of liberty cannot be reduced to a quantitative basis.

Steiner draws attention to another difficulty involved in attempting to compute the values of different liberties – that some of these values would presumably have to be negative, since some actions are actually of disvalue. For example, says Steiner, we cannot give a positive value to an act of killing, since if we did so it could mean that a sufficiently large number of acts of killing would be of greater value than one act of saving life. So acts of killing must receive a negative value. But computing negative values along with positive values leads to self-contradictory results. Suppose we add to a list of three actions, A, B and C, that Red is free to do, all of which have positive values, a fourth action, Y, which has negative value, the result would be that the numerical sum of Red's freedom would be reduced. 'That is, Red's newly acquired liberty to do Y would entail a *decrease* in his freedom.' (Steiner, 1983, p.81). Of course, an act of killing, although condemned by society, might be regarded by someone (e.g. the killer) as having positive value, and so from that perspective would not reduce the agent's freedom. So Steiner's analysis presupposes that we are guided by the judgements of society as a whole – by which, of course, life-taking is condemned. This further illustrates the difficulty of working with two different criteria of preferences/judgements – the personal and the social – thereby compounding the element of ambiguity in our calculations.

One solution to the problem raised by Steiner would be to exclude from the calculations all the actions that have been awarded negative values. But, says Steiner, this would mean that the basis of the formula would shift from a 'negative' concept of liberty to a 'positive' concept of liberty, since Red would be deemed not to be free in performing bad actions. For this reason Steiner concurs with Taylor's claim that the introduction of valuational weightings necessarily shifts us towards the 'positive' concept of liberty, but he demurs from Taylor's conclusion that this makes our acceptance of the 'positive' concept of liberty inevitable. On the contrary, Steiner's conclusion is that in order to stay within the 'negative' concept of liberty, we must abandon qualitative valuations, and count all freedoms as of equal value (Steiner, 1983, pp.82–3). But if we do exclude 'positive' liberty from the calculations, Steiner's insistence on treating all 'negative' liberties as of equal weight, seems arbitrary (Oppenheim, 1961, p.195). The conclusion that seems forced upon us is that while some account must be taken of the dimension of importance in any assessment of freedom, we cannot find a precisely measurable way of doing it.

4   The difficulty of performing actions

Many writers claim that freedom is partly a matter of degree. They argue that the extent of a person's freedom depends not only upon the number of options open or closed to her, and the importance to her of choosing those options (itself perhaps a matter of degree as well as of kind), but also upon the degree of difficulty she encounters in exercising that choice (Bayles, 1972, p.25). Berlin's second scale (b) is designed to measure this dimension of freedom; account must be taken, says Berlin, of 'how easy or difficult each of these possibilities is to actualise'. The inclusion of this scale is defended on the ground that an option which cannot be exercised without extreme difficulty contributes less to a person's freedom than does an option which can be exercised easily. This is to focus attention upon the conception of liberty in terms of effective power; my effective power is greater the easier I find it to exercise the options open to me; my effective power is less the harder I find it to exercise the options open to me. For instance, I may be free to watch either of two films, but if I can watch one of them only in London because it is banned everywhere else, whereas I can watch the other in any major British city, then, it is said, I am less free to watch the one film than the other.

However, Steiner and Day have dismissed the idea that freedom can be a matter of degree. According to Steiner (1983, p.78), there are no degrees of freedom to do something: either one has the freedom to do something or one does not have the freedom to do it. In the example of the two films, the position is simply that I am free to watch one of them in London but not elsewhere, while I am free to watch the other both in London and elsewhere. I am not less free to watch the one than the other: I am merely prevented from watching it in so many venues. There is no difference in the degree of my freedom, only in its extent: I am just as free to watch both films, but not in the same places.

In developing this argument, Steiner uses another example – that of a British passport holder who would be judged on Berlin's scale (b) to be less free than a Canadian passport holder to enter the USA, because the Briton requires a visa, but the Canadian does not. Steiner denies, however, that the Briton is thereby less free than the Canadian; the Canadian is free to enter the USA, and the Briton is either free or unfree to enter the USA, depending upon whether his visa is forthcoming or not. Of course, says Steiner, the process of obtaining a visa may entail certain prior actions which the Briton may be unable to perform. But this does not mean that the Briton is less free than the Canadian; if the Briton is unable to perform these prior actions, he is unfree (not less free than the Canadian) to enter the USA; if he is able to perform these prior actions, he is free (just as free as the Canadian) to enter the USA.

Steiner's argument is persuasive up to a point. But there does seem to be some enduring attraction in the idea of degrees of freedom, and Steiner himself admits that there is one sense in which it may be legitimately employed. This is the statistical sense in which it may be said that the Briton is less free than the Canadian because it is *likely* that the Briton will be prevented by the difficulties of obtaining a visa from entering the USA. (Steiner, 1983, p.79). This is to say, not that the Briton is less free than the Canadian, but only that he is more likely to be unfree. But is this all that the notion of degrees of freedom amounts to?

Even if Steiner is right to confine the notion of degrees of freedom to statistical probabilities of behaviour, is his conception of the relevant area of behaviour too narrowly drawn? Steiner confines attention to the probability of an agent being *prevented* from performing an action; but what of the probability of an agent being *deterred* from performing the action? Has X a lesser degree of freedom than Y if she is more likely to yield to threats of punishment for performing an action? The drawback with taking account of deterrence is that it implies that the degree of freedom is a function of the degree of imperturbability of the agent. (Scott, 1959, p.218). One way around this difficulty might be to contrast sanctions rather than agents – i.e. to say that the degree of freedom depends upon the severity of the sanction rather than upon the reaction of the agent. Hence, for example, a fine of £200 for a parking offence would be deemed a greater restriction on a motorist's freedom than would a fine of £10. But how can we separate the severity of the sanction from the reaction of the agent, for purposes of estimating degrees of deterrence? Some motorists may be deterred no matter how light the penalty for parking, while others may not be deterred no matter how severe the penalty (within reason). It seems hard to avoid subjectivity in any attempt to measure degrees of freedom in terms of probability of deterrence.

This brings us to a consideration of the practical problems involved in calculating degrees of difficulty. If we are to measure degrees of difficulty in performing actions, we must devise a scale for doing so. The obvious way to construct such a scale is to calculate the opportunity costs attached to different actions, on the assumption that the lower the opportunity cost of an action, the greater the freedom. But how do we *quantify* the opportunity costs of actions? Swanton (1979, p.345) suggests that we could construct an 'equivalence table', to map costs such as 'fines . . . imprisonment, bodily and mental harm, time and effort' etc. 'on a single scale', using 'money as a unit'. However, Swanton is somewhat optimistic in her assumption that very different types of opportunity cost can all be reduced to a single monetary scale. She refers to the practice of law courts, where 'prison terms are equated to certain fines'. But the enormous variations that we see in such legal calculations suggest that widespread agreement on a single scale of equivalences is highly unlikely.

Perhaps a statistical estimate of the probability of being prevented from doing something is easier to obtain? Steiner believes such an estimate to be a 'perfectly sensible statistical judgement', and Oppenheim (1961, p.187) is similarly sanguine. This notion of a statistical estimate of the ease or difficulty of performing actions leads us to the behavioural approach to the measurement of freedom pioneered by the Gabors.

5 The determinism of actions

The final problem faced by those attempting to measure freedom is raised by the fact that some actions may be determined by social causes outside the agent's control, thereby rendering the agent unfree in performing them. If we are to measure freedom, therefore, we must find some way of calculating the extent to which an agent's choices are her own. In effect, what is being proposed here is that we must take into account the conception of freedom in terms of self-determination.

The only writers to have attempted to measure self-determination are Denis and André Gabor. (Despite the fact that they present their analysis in terms of freedom defined as 'absence of undesirable restraint', it is clear that they are concerned only with restraints of a socially deterministic kind.) The Gabors have produced a so-called 'statistical approach' to freedom in which they set out to measure 'actual manifestations of freedom' (Gabor, [A.], 1979c, p.430). The Gabors' system is developed around two principles – diversity and independence. There must be some diversity in the choices made by the agent's peer group, otherwise that agent cannot be said to have any freedom; and the greater the extent of this diversity, the greater the agent's freedom.

'The extent to which a member of a group was free in choosing between a set of alternatives can be gauged by the extent to which the group as a whole availed itself of the variety of choices offered... If all the members of a group have made the same choice, they have not displayed any freedom in their actions, and if they have distributed themselves evenly over the several alternatives open to them, they have achieved the maximum degree of manifest freedom in the given situation.' (Gabor, [A.], 1979b, p.400)

However, even when there is diversity in people's choices, there may still be unfreedom, since that diversity may be induced by extraneous causes such as social pressure or authoritative commands. For example, diversity in voting behaviour may simply reflect class or occupational alignment, thereby exemplifying unfreedom. Hence, while it is a necessary condition, diversity is not a sufficient condition of freedom (Gabor, [D.&A.], 1979b, p.417). Freedom requires not only diversity, but also independence. It is not enough that people make diverse choices; they must make those diverse choices autonomously.

The Gabors propose, therefore, first to estimate the extent of diversity of choices, and second to estimate the extent to which those choices are independently made. The two resulting figures would then be multiplied together to yield a measure of the level of diverse behaviour which is independently chosen – and this is what the Gabors take to be freedom. So there is nil freedom where there is either nil diversity or nil independence, but in all other situations freedom has a positive value, and this positive value increases as the extent of diversity and/or independence increases (Gabor, [A.], 1979c, p.434).

So far as we are concerned, the main value of the approach to the measurement of freedom recommended by the Gabors lies in the help it can give in calculating the extent to which an agent's choices are determined by forces beyond her control. How helpful is it? It has been criticised on grounds that the principle of diversity measures the extent of the exercise or take-up of freedom (what people do with their freedom), rather than the extent of freedom itself (how much liberty people have). The Gabors argue that if people do not exercise a particular freedom, effectively it ceases to exist. 'We take the view that what the individuals "care to do" or "may care to do" must manifest itself in the actions of at least a fraction of the population' (Gabor, [D.&A.], 1979a, p.332). However, the fact that no one exercises a particular freedom does not in itself signify that that freedom does not exist, but only that people do not want to exercise it. In other words, the Gabors' principle of diversity seems to measure people's preferences rather than their freedom. People can persistently decline to do something, yet be free to do it.

One possible response to this criticism would be to say that the Gabors' scheme is a measurement of freedom defined as doing what one wants. If a person never exercises a particular freedom, we might interpret that fact as an indication that it is an option that she does not want, and therefore that it forms no part of her freedom (interpreted as want-satisfaction). However, the Gabors would not adopt this position, since they believe that behind the notion of want-satisfaction lies a deeper conception of freedom – that of self-determination. If, for example, a person's wants are the result of determining influences, then the satisfaction of those wants would not make her free.

The Gabors' own response to the criticism is to argue that, while there is a theoretical sense in which an option that is never chosen could still conceivably exist, in practice such an option remains a purely hypothetical possibility. The fact that no one *does* choose an option is *prima facie* evidence that no one *can* choose it.

'It is a fact of experience that wherever a free choice between genuine alternatives is offered to a large group... the decisions of its members will tend to differ, and it cannot be mere coincidence that both in Britain and in the United States government and opposition poll about equal numbers of votes in national elections... It seems that where there is true freedom present, it will tend to be exercised... a realistic measure of the extent to which an individual could have acted otherwise than he has actually acted is the extent to which other members of the group have *de facto* acted otherwise.' (Gabor, [A.], 1979a, pp.397,398)

So uniformity of choices is in itself an indicator of dependence; where everyone chooses in the same way, there must be some extraneous cause at work determining those choices. This is an interesting hypothesis, though difficult to substantiate (or falsify) because of its essentially deductive nature (despite its empirical presentation). But even if we accept the hypothesis that uniformity of choices necessarily entails the absence of self-determination, we face the problem of how to calculate the extent of self-determination in circumstances where diversity of choices does exist. Can we ever be certain that we are aware of all the relevant determining factors in a given case, still less of their overall impact on an agent's choices? Even trying to take into account a single determining factor may prove to be excessively difficult.

Conclusion on the measurement of freedom

Many difficult problems surround the attempt to measure freedom. The main problems arise in determining how to quantify liberties. What constitutes a liberty for purposes of quantification? Is there any common denominator between liberties by which we can reduce them to the same basic unit? If liberties differ in degrees of importance and of difficulty of exercising them, can we estimate these degrees in any precise fashion? If liberties differ in kind, are these qualitative differences beyond the capacity of measuring techniques to calculate? Can we estimate the extent to which our actions are determined by extraneous causes? Even if we can satisfactorily construct scales for measuring respectively, the number of options, the extent of obstacles, the importance of restrictions, the difficulty of performing actions, and the extent of human autonomy, how can we calibrate all of these scales on a single gauge? The foregoing discussion has served to clarify some of the issues raised by these questions, but our conclusion must be that any statement purporting to measure the freedom of an individual or country, or to compare it with the freedom of another individual or country, must be treated with extreme caution. This is not to suggest that such statements are meaningless or misconceived – i.e. that, as Faraday put it, 'If you cannot measure it, it doesn't exist'. It is to say that we must be prepared to accept that such statements about freedom cannot be interpreted as more than rough-and-ready assertions. But even rough-and-ready assertions may have validity; we make such assertions all the time in other spheres of life, with confidence that we are judging sensibly. Why should we not regard statements about the extent of freedom in the same light? Making a quantitative statement that there is more freedom in country X than in country Y is in principle no more problematical than making the common-or-garden statement that this man is balder than that man. Similarly, making the qualitative statement that the more valuable liberties are better protected in country X than in country Y is in principle no more problematical than making the common-or-garden statement that this woman is happier than that woman. The point is that we make comparative statements all the time in our everyday lives, and provided we do not demand from them a high degree of precision, there is no reason to dismiss them as unsubstantiatable. This is equally true of comparative statements about liberty.

Finally, the conclusion has emerged that measurement issues concerning liberty reflect, to some extent, issues about the meaning of liberty. That is to say, some of the difficulties of measuring freedom arise out of the fact that there are several different conceptions of freedom. For instance, the initial problem of delimiting actions (whether we must count both unfree and free acts) is a reflection of the contrast between the absence of impediments conception and the availability of choices conception of freedom; one of the problems of ranking freedoms in order of importance (that of dealing with freedoms of negative value) is a reflection of the contrast between the absence of impediments conception and the self-mastery conception of freedom; the problem of calculating degrees of difficulty of performing actions is a reflection of the contrast between the impediments conception and the effective power conception of freedom; and the problem of estimating to what extent our actions are determined is a reflection of the contrast between the availability of choices conception and the self-determination conception of freedom. Hence, the selection of a particular conception of freedom may well be more critical to the issues raised by the attempt to *measure* freedom than to the issues raised by the attempt to *justify* freedom. This may be less surprising than at first it seems, if we bear in mind that when we are trying to measure something, we must be clear precisely what it is that we are measuring, whereas when we are trying to justify something, we may well be able to accommodate a variety of different forms of that thing within the same justificatory argument. Measurement, in short, demands greater specificity than does justification.

5 Aggregation and Distribution of Freedom

The final area of inquiry into freedom raises issues of aggregation and distribution. The central question concerning the aggregation and distribution of liberty in a society is 'can the arrangements which affect freedom be managed to alter the overall level of freedom, or are we able only to alter the distribution of freedom?' On the *variable sum* view, it is possible to increase or reduce the overall level of freedom in society, and in general we should aim to maximise or at least increase that overall level wherever possible. On the *zero sum* view, we cannot alter the overall level of freedom in society, since one person's freedom is necessarily at another person's expense, and therefore the sum total of freedom is always constant (sums to zero). All that we can do is to alter the way in which freedom is distributed, and the aim should be to distribute freedom as fairly as possible. In this chapter, I discuss the coherence of these two sets of arguments. But, first, a note about the conceptions of freedom to be employed in discussing aggregative and distributive issues. At first sight, it would seem likely that the choices conception, the status conception, the self-determination conception and the self-mastery conception would each yield a variable sum view of freedom, since simultaneously everyone can have more choices made available to them, or have more civil and political rights, or become more autonomous, or develop more self-control. Conversely, at first sight, it would seem likely that the effective power conception would yield a zero sum view, since one person's power is necessarily at another's expense. As for the two remaining conceptions – absence of impediments and doing what one wants – each could yield a variable sum view, (in circumstances where people's actions or wants did not conflict), or each could yield a zero sum view, (in circumstances where people's actions or wants did

conflict). In what follows, however, we will see that the position is
rather more complicated than this. In discussing aggregative and
distributive issues, I will generally employ the four conceptions that
fall into the category of interpersonal conceptions of freedom,
together with the doing what one wants conception, since it is in
relation to these five conceptions that the most acute aggregative
and distributive issues are raised.

1 The variable sum view

This is the view that we can increase or reduce the overall sum of
freedom in a society. It is a view that is implicit in many comparative
judgements about freedom in different countries, and in the same
country at different times. For example, the opinion that there is
more (or less) freedom in Britain than in Albania, and the opinion
that there is more (or less) freedom in the United States in the 1980s
than there was in the 1880s, both presuppose the variable sum view
of freedom. It is also implicit in many assertions about the purpose
of governmental restraint, in that governmental intervention with
liberty in one sphere is often justified in order to protect it in another
sphere, the result being a net increase in freedom (Feinberg, 1980,
p.42). Variable sum theorists usually think in terms of such trade-
offs; rarely is there a suggestion that we can produce an increase in
freedom without at least some decrease in freedom. 'Even a law
which enacts that no one shall coerce anyone in a given sphere, while
it obviously increases the freedom of the majority, is an "infraction"
of the freedom of potential bullies and policeman' (Berlin, 1969,
p.xlix).

Such trade-offs may be cast in terms of a single liberty, or in terms
of two or more liberties. In terms of a single liberty, the trade-off
may be between doing, and preventing others doing, the same thing;
for example, it may be argued that I gain more freedom of action
from a law protecting freedom of worship than I lose by being
forbidden from preventing others from engaging in worship. Or the
trade-off may be between the reduction in freedom for a small
number of people, in order to secure an increase in that freedom for
a larger number of people; for example, the abolition of slavery
reduced the freedom of a comparatively small number of slave-
owners to control slaves, but increased the freedom of a

comparatively large number of slaves not to be controlled by slave-owners. In terms of two or more liberties, the trade-off may be between doing many things and being prevented from doing one thing; for example, I gain many kinds of freedom of action from a law protecting me from murder, but I lose only one freedom – the freedom to murder. Or the trade-off may be between a lesser freedom for one person and a greater freedom for another person; for example, Feinberg (1980, p.43) argues that rape laws restrict a lesser ('limited') liberty of men in order to protect a greater ('fecund') liberty of women.

However, in calculating such trade-offs, problems of comparing like with like may occur. In the above examples, what is being traded off may be a gain in security against a loss in liberty, or a gain in a more important area of liberty against a loss in a less important area of liberty, or a gain in liberty which is defined in one way against a loss in liberty which is defined in another way.

The variable sum theorist will normally want to *maximise* or at least *increase* the sum total of liberty in a society, other things being equal. The qualification, 'other things being equal', is important, since the variable view does not commit its holder to the doctrine that liberty is the only value, or even the most important value. All that the variable sum view necessarily entails is that overall liberty *can* be increased; not that it *must* be increased. The variable sum view is quite compatible with the judgement that liberty is less important than, say, moral welfare, and that an overall reduction in liberty is a price worth paying for a more wholesome society. This may be a justification for laws against pornography, for example (Feinberg, 1980, p.44, fn.13). But if in a particular case there is no value which is superior to freedom, then the variable sum theorist will seek to maximise or at least increase net liberty in society. Both of these objectives raise difficult issues, which we must now consider.

(a) Maximising liberty

The Deputy Leader of the British Labour Party, Roy Hattersley, is an advocate of liberty-maximisation:

'socialism's fundamental purpose – indeed, the purpose of the equality which we seek – is the extension of liberty... *It is a commitment to organise society in a way which ensures the greatest sum of freedom, the highest total amount of real choice* ... the

greatest good is the greatest freedom and . . . the only argument of
consequence is how it can be extended to the greatest number.'
(Hattersley, 1987, pp.21–2,130)

But O'Neill (1979/80, p.45) argues that the goal of liberty-
maximisation is 'indeterminate', since 'there is no general procedure
for identifying a largest (or a larger) set of liberties'. There are
innumerable kinds of trade-off between different liberties in society;
for example, between one person's freedom of speech and another
person's freedom to prevent speech; between the freedom of the car
driver and the freedom of the pedestrian; between the freedom of the
press and the protection of individual privacy. If liberty is to be
maximised, wherever there is conflict between freedoms, a decision
must be made as to which freedom must prevail. But how can we
possibly calculate which permutation or set of literally thousands of
trade-offs between liberties in society is the one that maximises
freedom? Perhaps the answer to this question is to select whichever
permutation of 'co-possible' liberties (i.e. liberties which are
consistent with one another) contains the most freedoms within it.
The difficulty with this solution is, however, that (as we saw in
Chapter 4) there is an element of arbitrariness in the way in which
we determine what is to count as a freedom; we can divide and
subdivide liberties to reach virtually any number we want. 'It would
always be possible to show that any given set of liberties was as
numerous as any other merely by listing the component liberties
more specifically' (O'Neill, 1979/80, p.50).

To circumvent this difficulty, we might select the Pareto-optimal
set of liberties – i.e. the set of co-possible liberties which contains all
the liberties which are contained in each of the other sets, plus at
least one additional liberty. The difficulty with this solution is,
however, that since many liberties are in conflict with one another,
no Pareto-set can exist, because conflicting liberties cannot (by
definition) be co-possible (O'Neill, 1979/80, pp.51–2). Perhaps the
set containing the most important liberties might be judged to be the
largest set. But the difficulties involved in determining what are the
important liberties (difficulties rehearsed in Chapter 4) include the
fact that we must employ some principle other than liberty (such as
utility or autonomy) to determine which are the most important
liberties. This either undermines the objective of maximising liberty
(as in the case of employing utility, since we would then be

maximising the value of liberty, not liberty itself), or merely transfers the problem of indeterminacy (as in the case of autonomy, since the conditions of autonomy are far from fixed) (O'Neill, 1979/80, pp.50–3).

These criticisms are concerned with the indeterminacy of liberty-maximisation. Liberty-maximisation has been criticised, however, not only for its indeterminacy, but also for its unfairness. Weale, for instance, has pointed out that it could mean the continuation of the institution of slavery in a situation where slave-owners outnumbered slaves (Weale, 1983a, p.56). Similarly, Crocker (1980, p.75) points out that liberty-maximisation could justify transferring resources from the disabled to the able-bodied, since handicapped people require considerably greater educational and medical resources than do non-handicapped people, to develop the capacity for exercising freedom. Of course, the liberty-maximiser could accept that in such cases the objective of maximising liberty must be sacrificed to the principle of fairness. As we noted earlier the variable sum theorist is not committed to the view that liberty should be maximised at any cost; the judgement that there may be some value, such as fairness, which in certain circumstances is prior in importance to the objective of liberty-maximisation, is perfectly consistent with the variable view of freedom. The point being raised here, therefore, is not so much a criticism of the variable sum view, as an observation concerning the general problem of weighing aggregative goals against distributive concerns.

(b) Increasing liberty

This is a less exacting goal than liberty-maximisation, and as such it avoids some, though not all, of the difficulties facing the maximisation principle. Showing that a policy results in an increase in liberty is obviously easier than showing that it results in the greatest liberty possible, but it raises similar technical issues of measurement and ethical issues of priority. I will examine these issues in the context of the ownership and distribution of private property, since there is a growing interest in the question of whether or not a change in the rules governing the institution of private property would result in an increase of freedom. In doing so, I am altering the emphasis of my analysis. Up to this point I have considered the variable sum issue in terms of the logic of the concept of freedom. Here I propose to consider it in terms of the empirical implications of applying the concept of freedom to a policy area. A change in the property rules may be extreme – i.e. abolition of the institution of private property – or it may be limited – i.e. redistribution of private property holdings. I will examine the issues of freedom raised by each of these changes in property rules in turn.

(1) The existence of private property. Variable sum theorists have different views on the question of whether the existence of private property enhances or diminishes freedom; the 'individualists' believe that it enhances freedom, the 'communitarians' believe that it diminishes freedom. According to the individualists, the notion of private ownership is inseparable from freedom. For example, 'self-ownership' – i.e. having a property in one's own person – is a precondition of being free, since without it, one is completely subject to the direction of others. It is a natural extension of this argument that having a property in one's possessions is also a precondition of being free, since without it, one lacks the material independence necessary to be able to resist other people's interference (Gray, 1986a, pp.62–63). On this view, private property is a bulwark against both *state* and *social* coercion. The fact that private property is a bulwark against *state* coercion, Lippmann (1934, pp.101–2) claims, can be seen by looking at Western Europe and the English-speaking world;

> 'What maintains liberty in France, in Scandinavia, and in the English-speaking countries is more than any other thing the great mass of people who are independent because they have, as Aristotle said, "a moderate and sufficient property". They resist the absolute state...There is no surer way to give men the courage to be free than to ensure them a competence upon which they can rely.'

The ability to mobilise any form of resistance to, or protest against, governmental action depends upon the possession of property (Ryan, [A.], 1987, p. 87). Private property is a *sine qua non* of the market system, and the market system is the means of preventing political authoritarianism from entering into economic life (Reeve, 1986, p.102).

However, these arguments are not wholly convincing. The institution of private property is certainly not a sufficient, and perhaps not even a necessary, condition for the prevention of political authoritarianism. There was an extensive system of private property in Italy and Germany between the wars, but that did not prevent the rise of totalitarianism (Ryan, [A.], 1987, p.87).

The argument that private property is a bulwark against *social* coercion is expressed by Gray in terms of the protection that it affords to individual autonomy. A private property-owner may do what he likes with his possessions, provided he keeps within the law; he is not constrained by the views or interests of his fellow-citizens. By contrast, under a system of communal property, 'if the individual's projects are ever to be realised in practice, they must be acceptable to the dominant opinion of his society or, at least, of the other members of his cooperative' (Gray, 1986a, p.65). Moreover, private property allows one to choose from whom to buy and sell, and thereby to evade the control of monopolists (Waldron, 1988, pp.300–1).

However, the claim that private property is a bulwark against social coercion has been much criticised. The critics argue that private property is itself a system of social restraints, in that every property-holding is exclusive to the holder, and therefore 'off-limits' to everyone else (Lloyd Thomas, 1981, p.179). Since other people are coercively prevented from using an owner's property, they are unfree with regard to that property (Loevinsohn, 1976/7, p.229). Accordingly, while each of us may be free in the use of *our own* property, we are all unfree with regard to the use of *everyone else's* property. If we sum these freedoms and unfreedoms respectively, we will find that the sum of freedoms is minuscule compared with the sum of unfreedoms; hence the system of private property creates vastly more unfreedom than freedom. The reason why this restrictive side of the institution of private property is so often ignored is that private property is seen by most people as an unalterable fact of life – a part of the social landscape akin to a natural phenomenon – and therefore as something that can only restrict ability, not freedom (Cohen, [G.A.], 1981, p.9). But quite obviously the institution of private property *can* be altered – indeed, the main anxiety of its defenders is that it may be interfered with; the fact that they resist proposals to abolish it indicates that they implicitly recognise that private property is not an unalterable institution.

Defenders of private property might, however, reply to this criticism by observing that under a system of communal property, it is only *theoretically* true that everyone is free to use and enjoy all the property in society. In *practice*, since only one person at a time can use any particular property, no one is any freer with regard to an occupied piece of communal property than they would be with regard to an occupied piece of private property. The net overall amount of freedom would not therefore be increased by the abolition of private property; only its distribution would change. Instead of the freedom to use a particular property being confined to a single individual (the owner), it would be conferred upon different individuals at different times, but only one at a time. While this means that freedom would be more equally distributed under a communal system of property, it does not mean that the total sum of freedom would be increased.

Critics of private property could, however, point out that under a communal system of property, the number of acts of use of property would increase, since there would be a much higher rate of usage of particular properties. Under a system of private property there is gross under-utilisation of property – there are long periods of the day (and night) when the owner vacates the property, and no one is using it. Such under-utilisation would cease or be reduced if private property were abolished, since as soon as one person vacated the property in question, another person could replace her. This is as true of commodities as it is of land or housing; private collections of books and paintings etc., limit effective usage much more than if they were in public libraries and museums. Cohen gives the example of tools and equipment – under private ownership equipment may only be used by its owner or by persons to whom that owner has granted permission; but under a communal system anyone could use any equipment not being used. This would increase tool-using freedom (Cohen, [G.A.], 1979, pp.1–7; Taylor, [M.], 1982 pp.154–5). If it is argued that the loss of previous certainty of access to property renders the freedom of access to communal property purely hypothetical – since if I have to wait my turn before being able to use some property, then effectively I have no freedom with respect to this property – the reply is that such an argument is fallacious; it is akin to asserting that I am unfree to use the telephone because the lines may sometimes be engaged (Gray, 1986b, p.166). We will return to this issue when we consider the zero sum view of the distribution of freedom.

Defenders of private property have argued, nevertheless, that there are three respects in which private property uniquely secures freedom – only under a system of private property can individuals have total control over property; only privately-held property guarantees privacy; and only private ownership generates a sense of status. On the issue of control, it is claimed that private owners have power of what Honoré has dubbed 'full individual ownership' over their property – i.e. completely unfettered control, including not only the rights of access and use, but also the right of disposal – whereas communal owners have only a fractional share in the control exerted over property by collective decisions. However, this contrast may be exaggerated, since much modern private property ownership is circumscribed by countless financial, legal and technical restrictions designed to protect the interests of others.

The defender of private property may, however, reply by drawing attention to the fact that so-called 'communal' property may not lie genuinely under the control of the whole community, but may be controlled by the state or government. In such circumstances (state socialism), the government possesses immense power over its citizens, and correspondingly threatens their freedom to a serious extent. For some writers this was the principal source of unfreedom in communist bloc states.

On the issue of privacy, it is often claimed that only under a system of private property is an Englishman's home his castle (Waldron, 1988, pp.295–6). Communal property provides no guarantee of privacy, since no one can be refused access to communal property. However, once more the contrast may be overdrawn; the private property owner cannot refuse entry to a host of public officials. Moreover, for as long as an occupant is using the communal property, there is no reason to assume that she enjoys less privacy than would be enjoyed by an owner-occupier.

Finally, on the issue of status, it is claimed by defenders of private property that only private ownership can confer the status of being free (Ryan, [A.], 1983, p.219). Without private property we are without anchorage, cast adrift in a world where our future is precarious and uncertain. With private property we have a stake in the world; it supplies both personal security and social recognition, giving us a sense of identity. Our property is, as Hegel puts it, the 'objectification' of our will; a concrete manifestation of the human spirit. We invest our personalities in our property – it is an extension of ourselves – 'we own therefore we are'.

However, these claims have been questioned by critics who argue that the legal status of ownership (being free in an institutional sense) conceals a real condition of alienation (being unfree in a psychological sense). Far from liberating its owner, private property imposes shackles on her (Kohr, 1974, p.52). The anxieties of owning property, which may include a constant sense of insecurity lest market conditions wipe out its value, together with the ties it imposes, including the expenditure of time and energy spent in accumulating and looking after it, mean that people may become instruments of their property rather than its master. Moreover, the materialism that private property engenders, and the competitive ethic it spawns, result in property owners' estrangement from both their own spiritual essence and their fellow citizens. Private property may thus be a self-enslaving or a self-alienating institution. Communal property would remove all these insecurities by separating well-being from possessions, and by conferring the status of freedom upon individuals as persons or equal citizens, rather than as wealth-holders.

What conclusion do we reach on the question of whether the institution of private property enhances or diminishes liberty? Clearly there are some respects in which private property enhances freedom – e.g. by giving the owner greater economic independence – but there are also some respects in which private property diminishes freedom – e.g. by reducing access and use. The answer to the question depends, therefore, upon how we evaluate these respective gains and losses. If we judge economic independence to be a more extensive or a more important freedom than access or usage, then we will conclude that private property on balance enhances liberty; but if we judge access and usage to be more extensive or more important kinds of freedom than economic independence, then we will conclude that private property on balance diminishes liberty.

(2) The distribution of private property. Since the institution of private property is increasingly well entrenched in contemporary societies, a more realistic issue dividing variable sum theorists

concerns its distribution rather than its existence. Defenders of the existing distribution argue against redistribution on grounds that redistribution is a gratuitous act of coercion against property-owners, i.e. it introduces coercion where there was no coercion before. Friedman (1962, p.174), for instance, claims that redistribution is inherently incompatible with freedom, in that it brings compulsory transfers into a situation where there were previously only voluntary (i.e. free) transfers through the market system. However, Friedman ignores the fact that the market system of voluntary exchanges itself constitutes a situation of unfreedom, in the sense that everyone within the market is confronted with a series of prohibitions on what they can do.

> 'Redistribution does not pre-empt or replace such voluntary exchanges. Rather it adjusts the structure of freedoms and unfreedoms from which people enter into voluntary exchanges. Thus the relevant comparison is not between voluntary exchanges and coercive transfers, but between the distribution of freedoms and unfreedoms with and without redistribution.' (Jones, 1982, p.229)

Whether redistribution results in a loss of freedom, therefore, cannot be taken for granted, but depends upon a comparison of the new set of freedoms and unfreedoms, with the old set of freedoms and unfreedoms.

Friedman may, however, insist that there is a crucial distinction as far as freedom is concerned between being coerced into doing something (being forced to pay taxes), and being prevented from doing something (being excluded from other people's property) – only the former entails unfreedom. To substantiate this distinction, Hayek (1960, pp.21,153) differentiates particular commands, which are discriminatory and cannot be escaped, from impersonal laws, which apply to all and whose sanctions can be avoided by not breaking them. Commands force us to act not upon our own plans, 'but to serve the ends of another', whereas in obeying laws, 'we are not subject to another man's will and are therefore free'.

However, the critics argue that any distinction between a law, which does not reduce freedom, and a command, which does reduce freedom, is untenable. Laws which protect property rights prevent people from doing things in just as effective a fashion as do redistributive measures (Loevinsohn, 1976/7, p.229). Being prevented from doing something is equivalent to being forced to do something, in the sense that one is being forced to not do something. In relation to freedom interpreted as absence of impediment, there is no categorical distinction to be drawn between prevention and coercion; both result in unfreedom.

An alternative formulation of the argument against redistribution is expressed in terms of the Nozickian charge that redistribution violates the rights of property-owners and therefore reduces liberty (Nozick, 1974, p.168). By taking away part of someone's property, the government is interfering with the material embodiment of that person's freedom – with their moral rights or objectified will – without in any way protecting anyone else's freedom. By transferring that confiscated property to someone else, the government does not increase *their* freedom, since the property in question is not and cannot be an embodiment of *their* will or rights, because it was not acquired legitimately (Jones, 1982, pp.220–1).

However, this argument only makes sense on two normative assumptions; that freedom is reduced only when rights are violated; and that property-owners have a right to keep their property intact. On the first assumption, a person is unfree only when unjustifiably interfered with. But this entails, for example, that a 'murderer is not rendered unfree even when he is justifiably convicted', whereas the truth is that 'even justified interference reduces freedom' (Cohen, [G.A.], 1981, p.10). Freedom may be reduced even when no right has been violated. The second assumption, that people have an absolute moral right to the property they legally own, has been challenged on the ground that it overlooks the moral claims of non-owners. Loevinsohn, for instance, argues that the root of the right of property-holders to their property is a prima-facie right of everyone to act in the way they desire to act; this right is one that necessarily extends to non-property-holders. Both property-holders and non-property-holders want to consume the goods in question, but the government prevents the latter from doing so, and thereby violates their prima-facie right (Loevinsohn 1976/7 p 231). In any case, the argument shifts the basis of the discussion from the issue of freedom itself to the issue of rights (Jones, 1982, p.222; Ryan, [C.C.], 1976/7, p.132).

If we put to one side such normative considerations, and concentrate upon the issue of freedom itself, by employing an empirical notion of freedom, it seems incontrovertible that any loss of freedom caused by redistribution must result in a corresponding gain in freedom. Suppose a sum of money is transferred from *A* to *B* by a third party, then 'if freedom is defined empirically and if it is appropriate to say that *A*'s loss of that resource constitutes a loss of freedom, then it must be equally appropriate to say that *B*'s gain constitutes a gain in freedom' (Jones, 1982, p.222–23). Whether or not *B*'s gain in freedom is greater than, smaller than or equal to *A*'s loss of freedom, is, however, less clear. Loevinsohn argues that if *B* is poorer than *A*, then *B*'s gain in freedom is greater than *A*'s loss of freedom, since the wants of the rich that are frustrated by property transfers are less extensive than the desires of the poor that are satisfied as a result of such transfers (Loevinsohn, 1976/7, p.234). However, this may not be true, since the extent of a person's unsatisfied desires is not necessarily correlated with the extent of their property-holdings; a rich person may experience more frustration of desires from losing property than a poor person may experience alleviation of frustration from gaining that property.

Loevinsohn seems on stronger ground when he switches from the conception of liberty as doing what one wants, to that of effective power, to argue that 'by transferring property from richer to poorer persons it would be possible to ensure wider access to certain critical goods and services such as food, medical care, education, transportation and means of communication. This would increase the range of people's opportunity, which would, on the broader conceptions of liberty, increase people's liberty' (Loevinsohn, 1976/7, p.238). However, it could be argued that the overall amount of freedom remains unaltered, and that all that changes is the distribution of access to this amount; proportionately more poorer people than richer people will now enjoy greater access than before to this fixed amount of freedom.

Perhaps the point that Loevinsohn is making is that the new options gained by the poor as a result of the transfer are more important than the old options lost by the rich. But who is to say whether the new options available to the poor *are* more important than the old options closed to the rich? Would the rich agree with this assessment? In any case, the issue has shifted from that of whether liberty has been increased, to that of whether the value of liberty has been increased (Jones, 1982, p.227).

There is one form of property redistribution that seems unequivocally to result in a reduction of freedom – that of taxing the rich to provide benefits in kind to the poor. In this case there is a net loss of freedom because benefits in kind remove the element of choice that cash benefits provide (Jones, 1982, p.219). Of course, there is nothing inconsistent with the variable sum view in this, since all that the variable sum view entails is that the sum of liberty in a society may vary – and this variation may be either in a downward direction (as in this case of redistribution), or in an upward direction (as is claimed in other cases of redistribution). Moreover, the variable sum theorist might welcome this form of redistribution, even though it reduces freedom, on the ground that in this case, welfare considerations outweigh considerations of freedom.

However, a zero sum theorist would dispute the conclusion that in this case (or indeed in any other case) there is a reduction in freedom, by drawing attention to the fact that one factor in the equation is the freedom of government itself – i.e. the freedom of ministers, civil servants and law enforcement officers to interfere with the lives of citizens. On the zero sum view, by taking this fact into account, we will find that the result of any property transfer must be neither an increase nor a reduction in the level of overall freedom, but only an alteration in the way in which the constant amount of freedom in society is distributed. It is to the rationale lying behind this assertion that we must now turn.

2   The zero sum view

The zero sum view is that we cannot alter the overall extent of freedom in society; all we can do is to alter its distribution. This is because one person's freedom is always at another person's expense; 'freedom for the pike is death for the minnows' (Tawney, 1964, p.164). In every society the aggregate of freedoms always sums to zero, and as a result, no society can be judged to be freer than any other, nor can a society be freer at some times in its history than at other times. Comparisons of freedom in societies can only take the form of comparing the way in which freedom is distributed within them. Steiner is the leading exponent of the zero sum view:

'The concept of liberty . . . is such that it makes no sense to speak of it as being enlarged or diminished – much less, maximised or minimised – within a society, but only as being distributed in a certain way . . . we can assess societies only in terms of their interpersonal distributions of liberty and not in terms of their aggregate amounts of liberty.' (Steiner, 1980, pp.245–6)

Only if one society is subjugated to another is there any exception to this rule, since, in such a situation, the subjugated society is clearly less free than the subjugating society. But this exception does not necessarily undermine the zero sum view, since if we consider the international community as a whole, we could argue that there is a fixed sum of freedom within *it* (just as there is a fixed sum of freedom within a hermetically sealed society), and that some countries secure more of that fixed sum of freedom than do other countries (just as within a hermetically sealed society some persons capture more than do other persons of the fixed sum of freedom that exists within their society). Of course, this assumption of a fixed sum of liberty in the world system could be challenged. The variable sum theorist could argue that just as liberty can be increased/reduced within a society, so liberty can be increased/ reduced in the world as a whole. For example, it could be claimed that during periods of colonialism, net liberty in the world is reduced (because those oppressed outnumber those oppressing them), while during periods of decolonialism, net freedom in the world is increased. Whether or not we accept this interpretation of colonialism/decolonialism, the point is that there is nothing in principle that distinguishes the situation of a hermetically sealed society from a whole world situation – arguments for and against the zero sum view apply equally to both. Let us now consider those arguments in some detail.

The basis of Steiner's zero sum analysis lies in his definition of unfreedom; he argues that if A is unfree to do P, this must be because some other person (B) is doing Q, which physically rules out the possibility of A doing P. It is not possible for both P and Q to occur; if Q occurs, then P cannot occur; if P occurs, then Q cannot occur. Where there is a constraint, the loss of freedom for some person(s) exactly matches the gain of freedom for some other person(s). Hence 'there can be no such thing as an absolute loss of (or gain in) individual liberty' (Steiner, 1974/5, p.50).

At first sight, however, it seems counter-intuitive to maintain that wherever there is a constraint, the loss of freedom to some persons exactly matches the gain in freedom to others. Let us see how Steiner's theory would deal with three awkward examples. Suppose a prison officer prevents 2000 prisoners from leaving their cells; on the Steinerian view, since *'freedom is the personal possession of physical objects'* (Steiner, 1974/5, p.48), the prison officer's exclusive possession of the prison corridors constitutes both her freedom and the unfreedom of the 2000 prisoners (since her possession of the corridors denies them access to that space). So the freedom of this single officer exactly matches the aggregate unfreedom of the 2000 prisoners. The second illustration is Steiner's own (1980, pp.244–45) – that of the emancipation of slaves. Emancipation did not, he says, result, as we might have supposed, in an increase in overall liberty, since it freed slaves from legal restraint only at the expense of an equivalent legal freedom of slave-owners to control them. The result may have been (was) a fairer distribution of freedom, but not a net increase in it. The third illustration involves the freedom of governmental officials; suppose that a government abolished the freedom to choose private health care; such a measure reduces the freedom of everyone in the state, but whose freedom does it correspondingly increase? On the Steinerian view, it increases the freedom of governmental officials *pari passu* by conferring upon them new powers of control over other people.

However, the Steinerian zero sum view is subject to three criticisms. The first criticism is that Steiner sometimes shifts the definition of freedom from that of power over *things*, to that of power over *persons*. The definition of freedom as power over things (the conception of freedom as effective power), does not necessarily imply a zero sum game, since (as we shall see shortly), there are circumstances in which we can all gain simultaneously an increase in our power over things. By shifting to a definition of freedom as power over persons, however, Steiner can argue more convincingly for a zero sum game, since power over persons is undoubtedly zero sum – in that A's power over B is necessarily at the expense of B's power over A and vice versa. But while the conception of freedom as power over things is coherent (as we saw in Chapter 2), the definition of freedom as power over persons is not coherent. If A exercises power over B, that means that B is thereby made less free (since B is being prevented from doing something), but it does not mean that *A* is thereby made more free. We would not normally say that enslaving someone increases the slave-owner's freedom, though it certainly decreases the slave's freedom. In what way is *A* freer than before she exercised power over *B*? How does *A*'s power over *B* make *A* free at all? Of course, *A*'s exercise of power over *B* prevents *B* from exercising power over *A*, i.e. it prevents *A* from being made unfree by *B*. But this seems a weak form of freedom for *A* compared to the strong sense of unfreedom for *B*. This imbalance becomes clear if we consider the example of the government's abolition of private health care; it is not a very compelling argument to say that the enforcers of this restriction become freer than they were before, because they can now prevent the population from coercing them in some way (in what way was the population coercing law enforcement officers before the abolition of private health care took place?). Still less is it convincing to say that the law enforcers' enhanced freedom exactly matches the reduced freedom of the population at large. The fact is that the law enforcers gain power over others, but not freedom; while the population loses freedom but not power over others. Steiner is not comparing like with like; he is comparing the gain of power over people by some, with the loss of freedom by others.

However, an alternative way of making sense of the claim that *A*'s exercising power over *B* is a means of enhancing *A*'s freedom is to employ the conception of freedom as doing what one wants. By exerting power over someone, I may be able to increase the extent of my desire-satisfaction (if only to gratify the desire to dominate that other person), and thereby attain more freedom, interpreted as doing what one wants. However, this would only yield the zero sum outcome asserted by Steiner if we assume that the gain in my desire satisfaction is exactly matched by a corresponding loss in desire-satisfaction experienced by the person over whom I exert power. But why should we accept such an assumption? The increased drive-satisfaction (if any) that I experience in coercing someone, may be larger or smaller than the reduced desire-satisfaction (if any) that is experienced by the person I coerce. The outcome of the exercise of power over people may, therefore, be one of variable, rather than zero, sum – more, or less, net desire-satisfaction, rather than a redistribution of a constant sum of desire-satisfaction.

Perhaps if we employ the conception of freedom as availability of choices, we can substantiate the zero sum view? On this conception, the possession of power by *A* over *B* may be interpreted as providing *A* with an option; *A* has the option of making *B* perform certain actions. Conversely, *B* is deprived of an option, since she cannot not perform any action commanded by *A*. In this sense, there is a symmetry in the freedom enjoyed by *A* and the unfreedom suffered by *B*: whenever *A* avails himself of the option to command *B* to perform an action, *B* loses the option to do anything else. This argument depends, however, upon measuring freedom in terms of act-types, rather than individual actions. That is to say, the act-type of *A* commanding *B*, and the act-type of *B* performing the command of *A*, are symmetrically equivalent. But in terms of the individual actions that *A* and *B* can perform, there is no such symmetrical equivalence since *A gains one option* (that of commanding *B* to perform an act), whereas *B loses all other options* (i.e. all options save that of performing the act commanded by *A*).

This is the substance of the second criticism of the Steinerian zero sum view – that it only makes sense if we count freedom in terms of act-types. For instance, in the prison example, the prison officer is the only person who can walk along the corridors, so she possesses the sole and entire freedom with respect to that type of act. If she released one prisoner, on the Steinerian analysis that prisoner would share equally with her the freedom to walk along the corridor, and both of them would have 1/2 of this act-type of freedom. If she released all 2000 prisoners, then she would share with all of them the freedom to walk along the corridor, and each would have 1/2001th of this act-type of freedom. However, if, instead of counting freedom in terms of act-types, we count freedom in terms of actions of individual persons, we would conclude that the unfreedom of the locked-up prisoners is 2000 times greater than the freedom of the prison officer, since if they were released, all of them would be able to walk along the corridors. Hence whether or not we adopt a zero sum view or a variable sum view depends in part upon how we count freedoms, by act-types or by individual actions. The difficulties involved in each of these alternatives were rehearsed in Chapter 4.

The third criticism of Steiner's argument is that in so far as it defines freedom as possession of physical objects (power over things) it unrealistically assumes both that all resources are in fixed supply, and that all resources are continuously possessed. Some resources are not in fixed supply. Suppose, for example, an expanding economy in which commodities are increasing in number and everyone is becoming richer; in such a situation no person's gain in possession of physical objects is necessarily at any other person's expense, and the society as a whole is becoming freer, both on Steiner's definition of freedom as possession of physical objects, as well as on other conceptions of freedom, such as availability of choices, and doing what one wants. Moreover, even when resources are in fixed supply, they are not always possessed at all times. As Taylor, ([M.], 1982, pp.153–4) points out in relation to a piece of property such as an open field, at a particular moment there may be no one occupying it, and in such a situation, everyone is free to use it. The obvious retort to this argument is to say that what Taylor has identified is merely theoretical or hypothetical freedom, since, as he himself acknowledges, as soon as anyone makes use of the object in question, no one else is free with respect to it. Hence it remains true that in practice only one person at a time can use the object; if A is using it, B is prevented from using it, and vice versa. However, there is a flaw in this retort. As we saw earlier, in our discussion of this issue when considering the variable sum view, Gray (1986b, p.166) points out that merely because we cannot all use the same telephone line simultaneously does not mean that we are all unfree with respect to the telephone system.

Accordingly, on Steiner's definition of freedom as the possession of physical objects, a system of shared use of physical objects would yield more freedom than would a system of private use. For example, if I share my six-roomed house with you, my freedom is not reduced by 50%, as Steiner implies, since I will always be free to occupy exclusively any one of at least five out of the six rooms, because you can only occupy one room at a time, and you may be out of the house altogether. Similarly, you will always be free to occupy exclusively any one of at least five out of the six rooms, for the same reason. Before I invited you to share my house, only one person (me) could with certainty occupy exclusively any one of all six rooms; now two persons can with certainty occupy exclusively any one of at least five rooms at any particular time. This suggests that the level of overall liberty has increased. There would be even more freedom if I invited some more people to share my house, as the following table indicates. On the assumption that exclusive occupation of a room counts as one unit of freedom, freedom will be maximised when I invite either two people or three people to share my house with me (making either three or four people in the house).

No. of persons in house	Units of freedom per person	Total units of freedom
one	six	six
two	five	ten
three	four	twelve
four	three	twelve
five	two	ten
six	one	six

Of course this also implies that if four or more people are sharing my house with me, total freedom would be increased by asking some of them to leave. Beyond a certain point, as the intensity of sharing increases, diminishing returns to liberty set in. But as Carter (1988, p.37) notes, 'while this argument implies that *making property more communal* (accessible to more people) can reduce freedom, it remains true that *making more property communal* will never reduce freedom'. In any case, whether total freedom is increased or reduced as the number of persons sharing the house alters, the situation is variable sum, not zero sum as Steiner's theory demands.

However, Steiner could reply that what he means by freedom is not mere occupation of, but control over, physical resources. Hence, if I invite you to share my house, I need not have to occupy a particular room in order to prevent you from making use of it; I may lock the door, or fill the room with boxes or instal a booby trap device. Accordingly, since there is a fixed amount of control over the rooms in the house, so there is a fixed amount of freedom with respect to the use of rooms in the house; I retain control (and therefore freedom) over all the rooms until or unless I allow you to exercise control over any of them, and if I allow you to exercise control over any room, I give up my freedom with respect to that room to you. Freedom remains zero sum.

In the sense that my having control over something entails that I have a permanent option to make use of that thing, Steiner's reply is convincing, since if we interpret freedom as availability of choices, it shows how my control over the remaining rooms in my house, after leasing one of them to you, could secure to me the option of using any of these remaining rooms, while denying to you that option. Hence the outcome is zero sum. Nevertheless, there is another sense in which my having control over something renders the outcome variable sum – if we employ the conception of freedom as effective power, and interpret effective power in terms of occupation. If I occupy one room and deny you access to another room, it is true that I am exercising control over both rooms, but I cannot *occupy* both rooms simultaneously; no one is occupying the second room. As a result of being unoccupied, the second room is not being possessed – although it is being controlled – and thus aggregate freedom, defined in terms of effective power interpreted as occupation rather than control, is less than optimal, and would be increased if someone were to occupy it. Hence the outcome is variable sum.

Whether one adopts a zero sum view or a variable sum view, therefore, critically depends upon which conception of freedom one employs, and how one interprets that conception. It also depends upon the particular circumstances under discussion. In some circumstances the absence of impediments conception of freedom suggests a variable sum view. For example, where a new law is introduced forbidding street demonstrations, there seems to be a net loss of freedom, since everyone is impeded by the new restriction, and only a small number of law enforcement officers are released from impediments preventing them from arresting street demonstrators. In other circumstances, the absence of impediments conception suggests a zero sum view. For example, where a new set of traffic lights is introduced, there seems to be no net loss or gain in freedom, since motorists can move through the traffic lights only at the expense of other motorists. Similarly, in some circumstances the availability of choices conception of freedom suggests a variable sum view – for example, where a disused theatre is re-opened, thereby making an option newly available to everyone – but in other circumstances the availability of choices conception suggests a zero sum view – for example, where one person's choice of marriage partner eliminates that choice for another suitor. Likewise, in some circumstances the effective power conception of freedom suggests a variable sum view – for example, where a rising standard of living enables everyone to make use of greater opportunities – but in other circumstances the effective power conception suggests a zero sum view – for example, in an auction room where only one bidder can obtain the good being auctioned. Similarly, in certain circumstances the status conception of freedom suggests a variable sum view – for example, where women are granted the suffrage along with men – but in other circumstances the status conception suggests a zero sum view – for example, where access to certain positions is necessarily restricted to an élite, as in membership of a legislative assembly. In the case of the remaining conceptions of freedom – the three intrapersonal conceptions – at first sight they all seem to suggest a variable sum view, in that we can all gain simultaneously in our capacity for self-determination (if, for example, some forms of social conditioning are eliminated); and we can all gain simultaneously in our desire-satisfaction (if, for example, costless improvements to the environment occur); and we can all gain simultaneously in the extent of our self-mastery (if, for example, we learn to be more moderate in our lives). However, there are circumstances in which a zero sum view can be entailed by any of these intrapersonal conceptions of freedom – for example, circum-stances of acute conflict in which the interest of one person or group is (or is perceived to be) diametrically opposed to that of another person or group. In these circumstances – as perhaps in Northern Ireland – one person's or group's capacity for self-determination, want-satisfaction, and even self-mastery, may depend upon that capacity being denied to another, rival, person or group, and thus the outcome is zero sum.

Equalising liberty

If we do adopt a zero sum view, what are its implications for public policy? Since, by definition, it cannot endorse a policy of maximising or increasing the sum total of freedom in society, it must confine itself to recommending a particular distribution of freedom. Steiner argues for an equal distribution of freedom – i.e. the equal liberty principle – and it is to an examination of this principle that the remainder of this chapter is devoted. But first it must be noted that there is no necessary connection between the zero sum view and the equal liberty principle. A zero sum theorist could propose an unequal distribution of freedom, say on perfectionist or on utilitarian grounds: for example, for the perfectionist reason that some people are better than other people or that their conceptions of the good are better than other people's (even Steiner does not propose equal freedom for persons who are not moral agents); or for the utilitarian reason that happiness, judged to be more important than equality, would thereby be promoted.

Moreover, the equal liberty principle could be adopted by a variable sum theorist. For instance, an equal distribution of liberty might be judged to be the means of maximising or increasing total freedom; or the objective of an equal distribution of liberty might be judged by the variable sum theorist, generally or in certain circumstances, to be fairer than the objective of maximising or increasing total freedom. Indeed, Weale (1983a, p.55) argues that this latter position is the standard liberal view. The typical liberal claims that since liberty is valuable, we have a greater obligation to ensure that everyone shares in it, than to aim at producing as much of it as possible (Crocker, 1980, p.75). However, unlike liberty-maximisation, liberty-equalisation cannot be derived simply from the fact that freedom is valuable. The case for liberty-maximisation rests on the fact that liberty is a good: if something is good, then it is better (*ceteris paribus*) that there should be more of it than less of it. Hence, if it is good that people should be free, it is better that they should be more free than that they should be less free. But when we have to consider how a good should be distributed, we have to refer to some principle external to the good itself. Hence, if I hold that freedom should be distributed equally, that relies upon my subscribing to a principle of equality, and not simply to the value of freedom (Goodin, 1982, p.154).

These considerations show that the principle of equal liberty, whether held by a zero sum theorist or by a variable sum theorist, must be justified and defended; unlike the liberty-maximisation principle, it cannot be taken for granted as a necessary deduction from the value of freedom. In the rest of this chapter, the main attempts to justify and defend the equal liberty principle are considered. There are two interpretations of the equal liberty principle; the 'specific' interpretation and the 'general' interpretation.

(1) the specific interpretation of equal liberty. The specific interpretation is that everyone should be free to do any act which does not prevent others from doing the same kind of act. Spencer (1851) interprets the equal liberty principle in this way. However, the specific interpretation has been criticised for its indeterminacy. It tells a government that it can only do to *A* what it can do to *B*, but it does not indicate what the government can or cannot do to both *A* and *B* (Gewirth, 1962, p.150). Provided *A* and *B* are treated equally

in respect of liberty, the principle is satisfied, irrespective of how much or how little liberty they both possess. Any particular restriction on liberty, and even a condition of general slavery, would be compatible with the specific interpretation, provided it applied equally to everyone. In other words, it does not entail any freedom at all; from the right to equal liberty interpreted in this way, we cannot deduce a right to freedom. It is worth noting that those variable sum theorists who have adopted the equal liberty principle (for reasons of fairness) sometimes try to deal with the problem of its indeterminacy by invoking a liberty-maximisation (or liberty-increasing) rule as a supplementary requirement. Hence, where there is a choice between two sets of equal liberties, we must choose the set that yields the greater amount of overall liberty. This is the position originally adopted by Rawls (1972, p.250) (though he subsequently withdrew the maximisation requirement, and with it, it seems, the variable sum view, enunciating a position that looks like the general interpretation of the equal liberty principle, together with a zero sum view (1981, pp.5,47)). But invoking a liberty-maximisation rule as a supplementary requirement does not rescue the specific interpretation of the equal liberty principle from the charge of indeterminacy. This becomes evident if we consider one of the implications of the specific interpretation – that it fails to protect people from acts of mutual coercion. The only actions that it rules out are actions by *A* that prevent *B* from doing the same. Hence, provided *A* leaves *B* in a position to retaliate in kind, *A* is free to assault *B*. So, for example, while it rules out murder (since murder renders the victim incapable of retaliating in kind), it does not rule out assault, or fraud, or libel, or any other injury inflicted by *A* on *B*, provided *B* is left in a position to inflict the same injury on *A*. Many writers have criticised the specific interpretation of the equal liberty principle for this implication, including Parsons (1892, p.5), Pollock (1981, p.20), Gewirth (1962, p.149) and Hobhouse (1964, p.36). The supplementary requirement that liberty should be maximised will not solve this problem, since a condition of mutual assault could be deemed to be one in which liberty is maximised.

(2) the general interpretation of equal liberty. The general interpretation of the equal liberty principle is that everyone should be free to act in any way that does not violate the basic liberties of other people (Gewirth, 1962, p.149). On this view, everyone has both

a right to be protected from coercion and a right to do anything that does not involve the coercion of others (Hart, 1967, p.53). The general interpretation of the equal liberty principle thus avoids the charge of indeterminacy by asserting a right of everyone to certain basic liberties.

However, this assertion of a universal right to basic liberties has been challenged on grounds that there is no satisfactory justification for claiming such a right. Several justifications have been suggested recently for the right to equal basic freedoms. Firstly, Rawls has argued on rational choice grounds that people in the original position would want to safeguard themselves from the risk of being denied equal basic freedoms, and would therefore choose as the prime principle of justice the equal liberty principle. However, critics have argued that it is not necessarily rational for someone to choose an equal distribution of freedom, because liberty may not always be welcomed if it is to be equalised; the opportunity cost that has to be paid for the benefit of an equal liberty may be too great (Hart, 1975, pp.247–8). When the veil of ignorance is lifted, we might find that we prefer to forgo a particular liberty for ourselves rather than to have to respect that liberty in others. For example, our desire to persecute others for their religious failings may be stronger than our desire to avoid persecution ourselves (persecuting others and, indeed, suffering persecution may serve important psychological needs, such as group identification and martyrdom). Since on Rawls's theory, we cannot know whether or not we have such preferences (the veil of ignorance prevents us from knowing our personal preferences when choosing principles of justice), we cannot know that it would be rational to choose protection of basic rights.

The second recent justification for the right to equal basic freedoms comes from Poole, who argues that it is a necessary condition of one person having certain kinds of liberties that others have them too. This is because the liberties of one person cannot exist in a vacuum, but depends upon the cooperation of others, and this cooperation in turn depend upon the freedom of others (Poole, 1975, p.12). For example, I cannot engage in political activity unless others do so too; hence if I am to have this freedom, other people must also have it. Accordingly, my range of basic freedoms presupposes an equal range of basic freedoms for others. However, as Poole acknowledges, not every basic freedom demands the cooperation of others. For instance, my freedom to walk along the seashore does not presuppose that everyone else has a similar freedom. Indeed, many of my freedoms (such as car driving) may be impeded by the like freedom of others. It might, however, be replied that my freedom to walk along the seashore *does* presuppose everyone else's similar freedom, since public access to the seashore is not secured for my exclusive benefit; I am only free to walk along the seashore because the seashore has been made accessible to everyone. Similarly with car driving; I could not drive my car at all unless roads were provided, and roads are provided to enable *everyone* to drive their cars. Hence my freedom to drive my car *does* presuppose everyone else's freedom to do the same.

Nevertheless, it could be argued that even if the liberty of *some* other people is necessary to make my freedom possible, such liberty need not be extended to *everyone*. To engage in political activity, for instance, I need the equal freedom of only some of the population, not everyone. An unequal franchise would provide the conditions under which political activity could take place, confining equal freedom to a small sub-set of the population – to those persons whose equal freedom is literally a condition of my freedom. Poole's reply to this criticism is to argue that any attempt to discriminate between those people who are literally necessary to my freedom and those people who are not literally necessary to my freedom is self-defeating, since by conferring a less-than-equal liberty upon the latter, I am permanently cutting myself off from engaging in activities that require their cooperation (Poole, 1975, p.13). In other words, in order to keep open my own future options, I must extend equal freedom to everyone. But why must I extend *equal freedom* to everyone in order to obtain their cooperation? I might be able to gain that cooperation by other means – say by financial inducement or persuasion. What Poole's argument lacks is a *moral* foundation – i.e. a reason why we *ought* to grant to everyone equal freedom.

Steiner's justification of the equal liberty principle supplies this moral foundation. Steiner (1974, pp.205–6) invokes the notion of the test of universalisability; if I claim a moral right to freedom, says Steiner, then I am doing so as a moral agent and therefore I am tacitly claiming a moral right to freedom on behalf of all moral agents. Accordingly, it would be 'unintelligible' for me to claim a more-than-equal freedom for myself, since that would entail the claim that all moral agents have a right to a more-than-equal freedom, which 'does not make sense'. Steiner's argument, however, only justifies equal freedom for moral agents; 'infants, the mentally ill etc.' are not, according to Steiner, moral agents, and therefore they are not entitled to equal freedom. In reply to the criticism that this opens the door to perfectionist and racialist arguments for less-than-equal freedom for those who are judged to be non-moral agents because of their mode of behaviour or genetic stock, Steiner has a decisive answer – that to deny anyone the status of moral agency is to absolve them from all sense of moral obligation to respect the liberties of moral agents. Hence the price that any moral agent must pay for the recognition by others of her own moral right to freedom, is her reciprocal recognition of the moral right to freedom possessed by those others. In support of Steiner's conclusion, we might add the observation that if perfectionists or racialists are going to deny that, for example, degenerates or Jews are moral agents, they must provide some convincing reason for that denial; their mere opinion on the matter need not impress us.

Even if the general interpretation of the equal liberty principle is satisfactorily justified, however, any attempt to apply it faces two difficulties. The first difficulty is that it fails to indicate what are the basic liberties to which everyone is equally entitled. Steiner (1980, p.249) claims that the equal liberty principle justifies the right to freedom from enslavement, because it confers the right to exclusive possession and use of one's own body, including one's labour, and a 'slave is a slave inasmuch as he lacks any such right'. But *how* does the equal liberty principle confer upon all moral agents ownership of their bodies? Perhaps Steiner's justification for the equal liberty principle itself – that the price of denying equal freedom to other moral agents is that they have no duty to respect my equal freedom – is tacitly employed to justify each application of the principle. Hence, in the case of enslavement, the reason why I must recognise that all moral agents own their bodies is that otherwise they will have no duty to recognise my ownership of my body. The difficulty with this argument is its *ad hominem* nature; it depends upon the values of the person employing it as to which freedoms she herself wants to claim. If she wants to claim a moral right to own her body, she must recognise other people's similar moral right, but if she does not want to claim such a right, then she need not recognise such a right in others. Similarly with all the other basic liberties – until and unless an agent wants to claim a right to any of them, she need not recognise a right of anyone else to them.

Perhaps the answer to this difficulty is that the basic liberties are those freedoms that everyone is agreed that they want to claim as moral rights. However, even if we are all agreed on the freedoms that we want to claim as moral rights, these freedoms may not all be compatible with one another. This is the second difficulty involved in attempting to apply the general interpretation of the equal liberty principle – that some of its implications may conflict. For example, if ownership of one's labour is an implication of the equal liberty principle, as Steiner claims, then this may conflict with the freedom to own private property. The conventional liberal view is that, far from conflicting, the freedom to own property is a *sine qua non* of self-ownership, since unless I have a right to own the property in which my labour is embodied, some other person could own that property, and thereby own my labour embodied within it, and this is 'tantamount to affirming the permissibility of slavery' (Steiner, 1980, p.250). But the fact is that private property can be inimical to the principle of self-ownership. For instance, private property in land could eventually result in the whole of the earth's surface being possessed by landowners, entailing the consequence that the non-owners were effectively in a condition of slavery to the owners, having no right to dwell anywhere without the permission of the landowners (Spencer, 1851, pp.114–15).

Steiner seeks to reconcile these contrary implications of the equal liberty principle by limiting the extent of the right of private property in order to make it consistent with self-ownership. For example, he argues (1980, pp.256,255) that 'the principle of equal liberty sustains no right of bequest', because 'the dead can have no rights against the living' – rights are attached only to living persons – and 'dead men cannot be slaves', so redistribution of their property cannot be said to violate the equal liberty principle. Steiner also argues that all resources must be appropriated on a temporary basis by leases of fixed duration, and that on the expiry of a lease (or the death of the leaseholder) any unconsumed resources revert to society for re-leasing. However, this interpretation of the equal liberty principle is challenged by more conventional liberal writers, who argue that the right of bequest is an integral part of the ownership of private property, and that the equal liberty principle guarantees such ownership in its entirety, without prejudicing the principle of self-ownership.

Clearly there is controversy over the way in which the equal liberty principle treats one freedom in relation to another in circumstances where they come into conflict. The point is that the equal liberty principle in itself is incapable of resolving these conflicts, since it implies that all the liberties which it endorses (and there is controversy about which these are, as we have seen) are sacrosanct. Only if there is designated some order of priority between them can such conflict be resolved, but any order of priority (such as that suggested by Steiner) must be derived from some value other than equal freedom, since the principle of equal freedom endorses mutually incompatible prescriptions (Gray, 1978, p.388). Just as we cannot decide *how* liberty should be distributed, without reference to some distributive principle separate from liberty itself, so we cannot determine *what* should be distributed, merely by reference to some distributive principle (such as that of equal liberty). We need an additional principle to specify *what* liberties are to be distributed equally, and in *what* order of priority. In other words, we require three principles; the first to justify granting people freedom; the second to determine how that freedom is to be distributed; and the third to specify which liberties are to be so distributed and which liberties are to take priority over others in the event of conflict between them.

Many problems are thus raised by the application of the equal liberty principle. Some of its implications are either unwelcome (the specific interpretation) or highly contested (the general interpretation). Nevertheless, for all its shortcomings, the equal liberty principle does seem fairer than the liberty-maximisation principle.

Conclusion on the aggregation and distribution of freedom

In answering the question of whether overall freedom can be increased, and if so, whether it ought to be increased, or if not, how ought it to be distributed, we have found that the *variable sum view*, which is implied in most comparative judgements about the extent of freedom, is the more plausible at first sight, though the objective of liberty-maximisation raises serious questions of both indeterminacy and unfairness. The weaker objective of increasing aggregate liberty was explored in relation to the institution and distribution of private property, and the conclusion was reached that some kinds of freedom were enhanced, but others were reduced, by the institution of private property, while on the issue of property redistribution, opponents of redistribution sometimes marred their case by employing normative views of freedom, and advocates of redistribution sometimes identified an increase not in freedom but in the value of freedom from property transfers. The *zero sum view*, though less plausible than the variable sum view at first sight – since it rules out the possibility of comparative judgements of levels of freedom in societies, and it entails that in every freedom-transaction the gains must exactly match the losses – can apply in some circumstances, and is often associated with the equal liberty principle, which is intuitively fairer than the goal of liberty-maximisation, if similarly ambiguous in its implications.

We have also found that the plausibility of both the variable sum and the zero sum view often depends upon the conception of freedom that is employed. Selection of a particular conception of freedom, and the way in which it is interpreted, may well determine the position taken on the variable/zero sum issue This conclusion – that one's conception of freedom is critical to one's response to issues of aggregation and distribution of freedom – is congruent with the conclusion reached in Chapter 4, that one's conception of freedom is critical to one's response to issues of measurement of freedom. It seems that we cannot separate the question of the meaning of freedom from the questions of how we measure it, whether it can be maximised, and how we ought to distribute it. By contrast, there is a much looser connection between the question of the meaning of freedom and the question of how liberty can be justified (as we saw in Chapter 3). It is interesting to speculate why this should be so; why should issues of measurement, aggregation and distribution of freedom be more closely linked than issues of justification of freedom, to issues of the meaning of freedom? Perhaps the answer is that measurement, aggregative and distributive issues are comparative in character, whereas justifica-tory issues are not, and comparative issues demand a high degree of particularity or precision in the thing being compared, whereas justifications can often be applied generally to a number of different interpretations of the thing being justified.

Summary and Conclusion

1 Summary

My purpose has been to explore the nature of the concept of freedom. I have attempted to do so firstly, in Chapter 1, by examining its meaning, concluding that there can be general agreement on the formal definition of freedom encapsulated in MacCallum's value-free formula that 'X is free from Y to do or be Z'. This is the root of the concept of freedom, the common denominator of all views about freedom, the framework within which every interpretation can be fitted. Where there is disagreement, it is over the way in which this concept is to be interpreted; in particular over the meaning of the three term-variables (X, Y and Z) in MacCallum's triadic formula. Such value-laden disagreements give rise to different conceptions of freedom – i.e. different interpretations of what the concept of freedom substantially entails, not disagreements about what it formally means. These different conceptions of freedom are many and varied in character, not reducible, as Berlin claims, to a simple division between a so-called 'negative' and a so-called 'positive' concept.

In Chapter 2, the seven major conceptions of the concept of freedom were examined, and I concluded that while none of them is without serious conceptual and practical difficulty, each of them captures something of what it is to be free, and effectively illuminates some aspect of this multi-faceted concept. Having shown what freedom is, and how it has been interpreted, in Chapter 3, I looked at the question of how it can be justified – i.e. why freedom is valuable. Six justifications were considered, none of which served to demonstrate that freedom in general was valuable, but each provided some support for particular kinds of freedom in different contexts.

In Chapter 4, the formidable problems raised by an attempt to measure the extent of freedom were examined – problems both conceptual (which conception of freedom do we use as the basis for measurement?) and evaluative (are freedoms commensurate, quantitatively or qualitatively?; can we weight for importance?). My conclusion was that any such calculations must be treated with extreme care. Finally, in Chapter 5, aggregative and distributive issues were discussed, including the question of whether liberty is a zero or variable sum concept, and whether the aim of public policy should be to maximise or to equalise freedom; the conclusion being reached that the variable sum view was more convincing than the zero sum view, but that the equal liberty principle was fairer than the maximisation principle.

2 Conclusion

One conclusion that emerges from this discussion is that we ought to treat with respect the different views of what liberty means and implies, since no view is flawless, and each of them supplies us with its own particular insight into this very complex concept. It is not convincing to seize on one conception and to claim that this is the real meaning of freedom. Nor is it helpful for a cold war to be conducted between advocates of so-called 'negative' liberty and advocates of so-called 'positive' liberty, since much of this conflict is a phoney war, founded upon conceptual confusion and exaggeration. It is much more fruitful to recognise that the many different conceptions of freedom are not necessarily in competition with one another, but serve to clarify different dimensions of an ambiguous concept. Nevertheless, we may legitimately select whatever conception of freedom we ourselves find most illuminating – indeed we *must* be discriminating if we are to apply the concept of freedom in practical discussion. Selection of particular conceptions of freedom, while not necessarily crucial to discussion of the justification of freedom (because many different justifications may be advanced simultaneously for any particular conception of freedom, and many different conceptions of freedom may be defended by a single justificatory argument), is crucial to the way in which freedom is to be measured, maximised and distributed. In this sense, the primary issue regarding freedom is that of how freedom is conceived, and hence the core chapter in this book is Chapter 2, where the seven conceptions of freedom are examined.

Another conclusion is that more research is required if we are to make progress in applying the concept of freedom. In particular, considerable analytical and empirical work is necessary in order to clarify and refine our understanding of the ways in which freedom can be measured and distributed. The current literature abounds with discussion (though sometimes aridly combative in nature) of the meaning of freedom, and there is increasing interest in the subject of the justification of freedom. But precious little effort has been devoted to the issues of the measurement and distribution of freedom. Yet comparative judgements concerning both the extent of freedom in different countries and the impact of governmental intervention upon the overall level of freedom and its distribution within a society are made confidently day after day, with little real grasp of the complexity of some of the issues involved. Since it seems that these judgements do play a role in important domestic and foreign policy decisions made by governments, it is a matter of some urgency that research is undertaken in order to place such judgements upon a sounder footing than at present.

Guide to Further Reading

In studying the *meaning* of freedom, the first essential is to read Berlin's 'Two Concepts of Liberty' (1969). Although Berlin's argument for dividing liberty into two concepts is controversial, the essay is a most stimulating account of freedom. MacCallum's article (1967), written to undermine the distinction between negative and positive liberty, is also required reading. On the issue of liberty as a value-laden or value-neutral concept, Cranston (1967) is particularly helpful.

The literature on *conceptions* of freedom is extensive. Beginning with the four interpersonal conceptions, helpful accounts of the absence of impediments view may be found in Parent (1974a), Day (1977), Miller (1983/4), Feinberg (1980) and Steiner (1974/5). The best defence of the availability of choices conception is by Benn and Weinstein (1971); it is criticised by Dworkin (G. 1982) and Parent (1974b). From different perspectives, Hattersley (1987) and Steiner (1974/5) enunciate the effective power view, while Feinberg (1980), Arendt (1961a & b) and Crick (1967) raise important issues concerning the notion of freedom as status.

Turning to the three intrapersonal conceptions of freedom, I have found Davis (W.H. 1971), Chisholm (1966) and Frankfurt (1971) most useful in illuminating the extreme version of self-determination (savaged by the extreme determinist, Skinner (B.F. 1973)), and I have found Campbell (1962) most useful in presenting the case for limited self-determination (criticised persuasively by Anderson (1981)), while Ayer (1946) is characteristically brilliant in undermining the attempt to reconcile freedom with determinism. The 'doing what one wants' conception is effectively analysed by Neely (1974), with helpful contributions from Dryer (1964), Smith (1977), Flathman (1987), Dworkin (G. 1970b), Frankfurt (1975) and Zimmerman (D. 1981b). Finally, on the conception of freedom as self-mastery, Dilman (1961/2), Green (1911), Scott (1956) and Maritain (1940) are all useful sources.

The *justifications* for freedom are far reaching. Suggestions for further reading include Benn (1971 and 1988) on presumption and rights; Raz (1986) on neutrality and autonomy; Ackerman (1980) and Jones (1989a) on neutrality; Dworkin (R. 1978), Hart (1967) and Steiner (1974) on rights; Young (1986), Lindley (1986) and Crocker (1980) on autonomy; Dworkin (R. 1978) on equality; and Mill (1975) and Schauer (1982) on utility.

The literature on the *measurement* of freedom is painfully thin. A useful starting point is Gastil (1987) and Humana (1986), in order to see measurement techniques at work. Steiner (1983) is by far the best analyst of the issues raised by comparative judgements of the extent of freedom, and Carter (1988) contributes some very shrewd insights into the problems involved. Feinberg (1980), Arneson (1985) and Taylor (C. 1979) also make useful contributions to this debate. Finally, the Gabors (1979) are the only writers to have examined the problems involved in measuring the extent to which our actions are determined.

Concern with issues of aggregation and distribution of freedom has been growing in recent years, though it remains an undeveloped area of analysis. Feinberg (1980), Swanton (1979), O'Neill (1979/80) and Crocker (1980) throw light on aggregative problems, while Jones (1982), Loevinsohn (1976/7) and Taylor (M. 1982) explore distributive problems. Steiner (1974/5, 1980) contributes effectively to both debates.

More generally, there are many useful articles on freedom in Griffiths (1983), Ryan (A. 1979), Friedrich (1962), Watson (1982) and Dworkin (G. 1970a). Oppenheim (1961) is the standard classic analysis of freedom as an empirical concept, while Weinstein (1965) presents a masterly short history of the idea of liberty in 19th century England. Finally, Cohen (1979, 1981, 1983) offers a left-wing perspective on freedom, while John Gray (1986b), Hayek (1960) and Friedman (1962) offer right-wing perspectives.

Bibliography

Ackerman, B. A. (1980) *Social Justice in the Liberal State* (New Haven: Yale University Press).

Aiken, H. D. (1962) *Reason and Conduct* (New York: Knopf).

Anderson, S. L. (1981) 'The Libertarian Conception of Freedom', in *International Philosophical Quarterly*, vol. 21.

Anshen, R. N. (1940) (ed.) *Freedom, its Meaning* (New York: Harcourt Brace).

Arendt, H. (1961a) 'Freedom and Politics', in Hunold, A. (ed.) *Freedom and Serfdom* (Dordrecht: Reidel)

—— (1961b) 'What is Freedom?', in *Between Past and Future* (London: Faber and Faber).

Arneson, R. J. (1985) 'Freedom and Desire', in *Canadian Journal of Philosophy*, vol. 15.

Arrow, K. J. (1972) 'Gifts and Exchanges', in *Philosophy and Public Affairs*, vol. 1.

Aune, B. (1962) 'Abilities, Modalities, and Free Will', in *Philosophy and Phenomenological Research*, vol. 23.

Ayer, A. J. (1946) 'Freedom and Necessity', in *Polemic*, vol. 5.

Bagehot, W. (1891) 'The Metaphysical Basis of Toleration', in *Literary Studies* (London: Longmans Green).

Banks, D. L. (1986) 'The Analysis of Human Rights Data over Time', in *Human Rights Quarterly*, vol. 8.

Bayles, M. D. (1972) 'A Concept of Coercion', in Pennock, J. R. and Chapman, J. W. (eds) *Nomos XIV Coercion* (New York: Atherton Press).

Belaief, G. (1979) 'Freedom and Liberty', in *Journal of Value Inquiry*, vol. 13.

Benn, S. I. (1971) 'Privacy, Freedom, and Respect for Persons', in Pennock, J. R. and Chapman, J. W. (eds) *Nomos XIII Privacy* (New York: Atherton).

—— (1975/6) 'Freedom, Autonomy and the Concept of a Person', in *Proceedings of the Aristotelian Society*, vol. 76.

—— (1988) *A Theory of Freedom* (Cambridge University Press).

Benn, S. I. and Peters, R. S. (1959) *Social Principles and the Democratic State* (London: Allen and Unwin).

Bibliography   177

Benn, S. I. and Weinstein, W. L. (1971) 'Being Free to Act, and Being a Free Man', in *Mind*, vol. 80.
—— (1974) 'Freedom as the Non-Restriction of Options: A Rejoinder', in *Mind*, vol. 83.
Benson, P. (1987) 'Freedom and Value', in *Journal of Philosophy*, vol. 84.
Bergmann, F. (1977) *On Being Free* (Notre Dame University Press).
Berki, R.N. (1968) 'Political Freedom and Hegelian Metaphysics', in *Political Studies*, vol. 16.
Berlin, I. (1969) *Four Essays on Liberty* (Oxford University Press).
—— (1980) *Concepts and Categories* (Oxford University Press).
Bernstein, M. (1983) 'Socialisation and Autonomy', in *Mind*, vol. 92.
Berofsky, B. (1966) (ed.) *Free Will and Determinism* (New York: Harper and Row).
Blackstone, W.T. (1973) 'The Concept of Political Freedom', in *Social Theory and Practice*, vol. 42.
Bronaugh, R. N. (1963/4) 'Freedom as the Absence of an Excuse', in *Ethics*, vol. 74.
Bronfenbrenner, M. (1954/5) 'Two Concepts of Economic Freedom', in *Ethics*, vol. 65.
Bryden, R. (1975) 'On Taking Liberties with Will', in *Philosophy*, vol. 50.
Campbell, C. A. (1962) 'Moral Libertarianism: a Reply to Mr. Franklin', in *Philosophical Quarterly*, vol. 12.
—— (1966) 'The Psychology of Effort of Will', in Berofsky *Free Will and Determinism*.
—— (1970) 'Has the Self "Freewill"?', in Dworkin *Determinism, Free Will, and Moral Responsibility*.
Carter, I. (1988) 'Maximal Freedom versus Property Rights: an Application of Action Theory', (M.A. (Econ.) University of Manchester).
Cassinelli, C. W. (1966) *Free Activities and Interpersonal Relations* (The Hague: Martinus Nijhoff).
Chisholm, R. M. (1966) 'Freedom and Action', in Lehrer, K. *Freedom and Determinism* (New York: Random House).
Cohen, G. A. (1979) 'Capitalism, Freedom and the Proletariat', in Ryan *The Idea of Freedom*.
—— (1981) 'Freedom, Justice and Capitalism', in *New Left Review*, no. 126.
—— (1983) 'The Structure of Proletarian Unfreedom', in *Philosophy and Public Affairs*, vol. 12.
Cranston, M. (1967) *Freedom: a New Analysis* (London: Longmans).
Crick, B. (1967) 'Freedom as Politics', in Laslett, P. and Runciman, W. G. (eds) *Philosophy, Politics and Society* (Third Series, Oxford: Blackwell).
Crocker, L. (1980) *Positive Liberty* (The Hague: Martinus Nijhoff).
Davis, M. (1978/9) 'The Budget of Tolerance', in *Ethics*, vol. 89.
Davis, W. H. (1971) *The Free Will Question* (The Hague: Martinus Nijhoff).
Day, J. P. (1970) 'On Liberty and the Real Will', in *Philosophy*, vol. 45.
—— (1977) 'Threats, Offers, Law, Opinion and Liberty', in *American Philosophical Quarterly*, vol. 14.
—— (1987) *Liberty and Justice* (London: Croom Helm).

Demos, R. (1940) 'Human Freedom — Positive and Negative', in Anshen *Freedom, its Meaning*.

Deutsch, K. (1962) 'Strategies of Freedom: the Widening of Choices and the Change of Goals', in Friedrich *Nomos IV Liberty*.

Devlin, P. (1965) *The Enforcement of Morals* (Oxford University Press).

Dilman, I. (1961/2) 'The Freedom of Man', in *Proceedings of the Aristotelian Society*, vol. 62.

Dodds, E. (1957) 'Liberty and Welfare', in Watson, G. (ed.) *The Unservile State* (London: Allen and Unwin).

Draughon, W. E. (1978) 'Liberty: A Proposed Analysis', in *Social Theory and Practice*, vol. 5.

Dryer, D. P. (1964) 'Freedom', in *Canadian Journal of Economics and Political Science*, vol. 30.

Dworkin, G. (1970a) (ed.) *Determinism, Free Will, and Moral Responsibility* (New Jersey: Prentice-Hall).

—— (1970b) 'Acting Freely', in *Nous*, vol. 4.

—— (1975) 'Paternalism', in Feinberg, J. and Gross, H. (eds) *Philosophy of Law* (California: Dickenson).

—— (1976) 'Autonomy and Behavior Control', in *Hastings Center Report*, vol. 6.

—— (1982) 'Is More Choice Better than Less?', in *Mid West Studies in Philosophy*, vol. 7.

Dworkin, R. (1978) *Taking Rights Seriously* (London: Duckworth).

Dybikowski, J. (1981) 'Civil Liberty', in *American Philosophical Quarterly*, vol. 18.

Elster, J. (1983) *Sour Grapes* (Cambridge University Press).

Esheté, A. (1982) 'Character, Virtue and Freedom', in *Philosophy*, vol. 57.

Fain, H. (1958) 'Prediction and Constraint', in *Mind*, vol. 67.

Fales, E. (1984) 'Davidson's Compatibilism', in *Philosophy and Phenomenological Research*, vol. 45.

Feinberg, J. (1980) *Rights, Justice, and the Bounds of Liberty* (Princeton University Press).

Ferré, F. (1973) 'Self-Determinism', in *American Philosophical Quarterly*, vol. 10.

Flathman, R. E. (1987) *The Philosophy and Politics of Freedom* (Chicago University Press).

Foot, P. (1966) 'Free Will as Involving Determinism', in Berofsky, *Free Will and Determinism*.

Fosdick, D. (1939) *What is Liberty?* (London: Harper).

Frankfurt, H. G. (1971) 'Freedom of the Will and the Concept of a Person', in *Journal of Philosophy*, vol. 68.

—— (1975) 'Three concepts of Free Action', in *Proceedings of the Aristotelian Society*, Supplementary vol. 49.

Friedman, M. (1962) *Capitalism and Freedom* (Chicago University Press).

Friedrich, C. J. (1962) (ed.) *Nomos IV Liberty* (New York: Atherton).

Frohock, F. M. and Sylvan, D. J. (1983) 'Liberty, Economics and Evidence', in *Political Studies*, vol. 31.

Fromm, E. (1942) *The Fear of Freedom* (London: Routledge and Kegan Paul).

Fuller, L. L. (1955) 'Freedom – a Suggested Analysis', in *Harvard Law Review*, vol. 68.

Gabor, A. (1979a) 'Freedom and Utility', in *International Journal of Social Economics*, vol. 6.

—— (1979b) 'The Concept of Statistical Freedom and its Application to Social Mobility', in *International Journal of Social Economics*, vol. 6.

—— (1979c) 'The Measurement of Freedom', in *International Journal of Social Economics*, vol. 6.

Gabor, D. and A. (1979a) 'An Essay on the Mathematical Theory of Freedom', in *International Journal of Social Economics*, vol. 6.

—— (1979b) 'The Application of Entropy to the Measurement of Social and Economic Freedom', in *International Journal of Social Economics*, vol. 6.

Gallagher, K. T. (1964) 'On Choosing to Choose', in *Mind*, vol. 73.

Gallie, W. B. (1955/6) 'Essentially Contested Concepts', in *Proceedings of the Aristotelian Society*, vol. 56.

Gastil, R. D. (1987) *Freedom in the World – Political Rights and Liberties 1986–1987* (New York: Greenwood Press).

Gewirth, A. (1962) 'Political Justice', in Brandt, R. B. (ed.) *Social Justice* (New Jersey: Prentice-Hall).

Gibbs, B. (1976) Freedom and Liberation *(New York: St. Martin's Press)*.

Goodin, R. E. (1982) 'Freedom and the Welfare State: Theoretical Foundations', in *Journal of Social Policy*, vol. 11.

Gould, B. (1985) 'Do Economic Constraints affect Liberty?', in *Socialist Philosophy Group Papers*, no. 1 (London: Fabian Society)

Gould, C. C. (1984) 'Self-Development and Self-Management: a Response to Doppelt', in *Inquiry*, vol. 27.

Graham, A. C. (1965) 'Liberty and Equality', in *Mind, vol.*74.

Gray, J. N. (1978) 'On, Liberty, Liberalism and Essential Contestability', in *British Journal of Political Science*, vol. 8.

—— (1980) 'On Negative and Positive Liberty', in *Political Studies*, vol. 28.

—— (1984) 'Introduction', in Pelczynski and Gray *Conceptions of Liberty in Political Philosophy*.

—— (1986a) *Liberalism* (Open University Press).

—— (1986b) 'Marxian Freedom, Individual Liberty, and the End of Alienation', in *Social Philosophy and Policy*, vol. 4.

Green, T. H. (1911) 'Lecture on Liberal Legislation and Freedom of Contract', in *Works* vol. 3 (London: Longmans Green).

—— (1921) *Lectures on the Principles of Political Obligation* (London: Longmans Green).

Griffiths, A. P. (1983) (ed.) *Of Liberty* (Cambridge University Press).

Haksar, V. (1979) *Equality, Liberty, and Perfectionism* (Oxford University Press).

Hampshire, S. (1965) *Freedom of the Individual* (London: Chatto and Windus).

Hancock, R. (1962) 'Ideas of Freedom', in *Review of Metaphysics*, vol. 15.
Handlin, O. and M. (1961) *Dimensions of Liberty* (Harvard University Press).
Hare, R. M. (1963) *Freedom and Reason* (Oxford: Clarendon).
Harris, C. E. (1977) 'Paternalism and the Enforcement of Morality', in *South Western Journal of Philosophy*, vol. 8.
Harris, N. G. E. (1972) 'Hart on Natural Rights', in *British Journal of Political Science*, vol. 2.
Harrison, G. (1975/6) 'Relativism and Tolerance', in *Ethics*, vol. 86.
Hart, H. L. A. (1963) *Law, Liberty, and Morality* (Oxford University Press).
—— (1967) 'Are there any Natural Rights?', in Quinton, A. (ed.) *Political Philosophy* (Oxford University Press).
—— (1975) 'Rawls on Liberty and its Priority', in Daniels, N. (ed.) *Reading Rawls* (Oxford: Blackwell).
Hattersley, R. (1987) *Choose Freedom, the Future for Democratic Socialism* (London: Joseph).
Haworth, L. (1979) 'Dworkin, Rights, and Persons', in *Canadian Journal of Philosophy*, vol. 9.
Hayek, F. A. (1960) *The Constitution of Liberty* (London: Routledge and Kegan Paul).
Hobhouse, L. T. (1964) *Liberalism* (Oxford University Press).
Humana, C. (1986) *World Human Rights Guide* (Sevenoaks: Hodder and Stoughton).
Husak, D. N. (1981) 'Paternalism and Autonomy', in *Philosophy and Public Affairs*, vol. 10.
—— (1983) 'The Presumption of Freedom', in *Nous*, vol. 17.
Jones, P. (1982) 'Freedom and the Redistribution of Resources', in *Journal of Social Policy*, vol. 11.
—— (1989a) 'The Ideal of the Neutral State', in Goodin, R. and Reeve, A. (eds) *Liberal Neutrality* (London: Routledge).
—— (1989b) 'Liberalism, Belief and Doubt', in Bellamy, R. (ed.) *Liberalism and Recent Legal and Social Philosophy* (Stuttgart: Steiner).
Jones, P. and Sugden, R. (1982) 'Evaluating Choice', in *International Review of Law and Economics*, vol. 2.
Kelman, S. (1981) 'Regulation and Paternalism', in *Public Policy*, vol. 29.
Kenny, A. (1973) 'Freedom, Spontaneity and Indifference', in Honderich, T. (ed.) *Essays on Freedom of Action* (London: Routledge and Kegan Paul).
Knight, F. H. (1941/2) 'The Meaning of Freedom', in *Ethics*, vol. 52.
—— (1947) *Freedom and Reform* (New York: Harper and Row).
Kohr, L. (1974) 'Property and Freedom', in Blumenfeld, S. L. (ed.) *Property in a Humane Economy* (La Salle, Illinois: Open Court).
Lacey, A. R. (1957/8) 'Freewill and Responsibility', in *Proceedings of the Aristotelian Society*, vol. 58.
Ladenson, R. F. (1975/6) 'A Theory of Personal Autonomy', in *Ethics*, vol. 86.
Lindley, R. (1986) *Autonomy* (London: Macmillan).
Lippmann, W. (1934) *The Method of Freedom* (London: Allen and Unwin).

Lloyd Thomas, D. A. (1981) 'Liberty, Equality, Property', in *Proceedings of the Aristotelian Society*, Supplementary vol. 55.

Loevinsohn, E. (1976/7) 'Liberty and the Redistribution of Property', in *Philosophy and Public Affairs*, vol. 6.

Lomasky, L. E. (1983) 'Gift Relations, Sexual Relations and Freedom', in *Philosophical Quarterly*, vol. 33.

Lukes, S. (1974) *Power: a Radical View* (London: Macmillan).

Mabbott, J. D. (1958) *The State and The Citizen* (London: Hutchinson).

MacCallum, G. C. (1967) 'Negative and Positive Freedom', in *Philosophical Review*, vol. 76.

Macfarlane, L. J. (1966) 'On Two Concepts of Liberty', in *Political Studies*, vol. 14.

Machlup, F. (1969) 'Liberalism and the Choice of Freedoms', in Streissler, E. (ed.) *Roads to Freedom* (London: Routledge and Kegan Paul).

Maritain, J. (1940) 'The Conquest of Freedom', in Anshen *Freedom, its Meaning*.

McCloskey, H. J. (1965) 'A Critique of the Ideals of Liberty', in *Mind*, vol. 74.

—— (1968) 'Some Arguments for a Liberal Society', in *Philosophy*, vol. 43.

Megone, C. (1987) 'One Concept of Liberty', in *Political Studies*, vol. 35.

Mendus, S. (1989) *Toleration and the Limits of Liberty* (New Jersey: Humanities Press).

Mill, J. S. (1879) *A System of Logic* vol. 2 (London: Longmans Green).

—— (1975) *On Liberty* (in *Three Essays*, Oxford University Press).

Miller, D. (1983/4) 'Constraints on Freedom', in *Ethics*, vol. 94.

Mulgan, R. (1984) 'Liberty in Ancient Greece', in Pelczynski and Gray *Conceptions of Liberty in Political Philosophy*.

Muller, H. J. (1960) *Issues of Freedom* (New York: Harper).

Neely, W. (1974) 'Freedom and Desire', in *Philosophical Review*, vol. 83.

Norman, R. (1987) *Free and Equal* (Oxford University Press).

Nozick, R. (1974) *Anarchy, State and Utopia* (Oxford: Blackwell).

O'Neill, O. (1979/80) 'The Most Extensive Liberty', in *Proceedings of the Aristotelian Society*, vol. 80.

Oppenheim, F. E. (1961) *Dimensions of Freedom* (New York: St. Martin's Press).

—— (1962) 'Freedom – an Empirical Interpretation', in Friedrich *Nomos IV Liberty*.

Parent, W. A. (1974a) 'Some Recent Work on the Concept of Liberty', in *American Philosophical Quarterly*, vol. 11.

—— (1974b) 'Freedom as the Non-Restriction of Options' in *Mind*, vol. 83.

Parsons, F. (1892) *Government and the Law of Equal Freedom* (Boston: New Nation).

Partridge, P. H. (1970) 'Freedom as the Possibility of Meaningful Choice', in Dewey, R. E. and Gould, J. A. (eds) *Freedom, its History, Nature, and Varieties* (New York: Macmillan).

Pelczynski, Z. and Gray, J. (1984) (eds) *Conceptions of Liberty in Political Philosophy* (London: Athlone Press).

Pitkin, H. F. (1988) 'Are Freedom and Liberty Twins?', in *Political Theory*, vol. 16.*

Plamenatz, J. P. (1968) *Consent, Freedom and Political Obligation* (Oxford University Press).

Pollock, L. (1981) *The Freedom Principle* (New York: Prometheus).

Poole, R. (1975) 'Freedom and Alienation', in *Radical Philosophy*, vol. 12.

Preston, L. M. (1982) 'Individual and Political Freedom', in *Polity*, vol. 15.

Rawls, J. (1972) *A Theory of Justice* (Oxford University Press).

—— (1987) 'The Basic Liberties and their Priority', in McMurrin, S. M. (ed.) *Liberty, Equality and Law* (Utah University Press).

Raz, J. (1986) *The Morality of Freedom* (Oxford: Clarendon).

Reed, G.F. (1980) 'Berlin and the Division of Liberty', in *Political Theory*, vol. 8.

Reeve, A. (1986) *Property* (London: Macmillan).

Rhees, R. (1969) *Without Answers* (London: Routledge and Kegan Paul).

Rousseau, J. J. (1963) *Emile* (London: Dent).

—— (1973) *The Social Contract* (London: Dent).

Rummel, R. J. (1983) 'Libertarianism and International Violence', in *Journal of Conflict Resolution*, vol. 27.

Ryan, A. (1965) 'Freedom', in *Philosophy*, vol. 40.

—— (1975) 'Liberty', in *New Society*, 13 November.

—— (1979) (ed.) *The Idea of Freedom* (Oxford University Press).

—— (1987) *Property* (Open University Press).

Ryan, C. C. (1976/7) 'Yours, Mine, and Ours: Property Rights and Individual Liberty', in *Ethics*, vol. 87.

Saunders, J. T. (1968) 'The Temptations of "Powerlessness"', in *American Philosophical Quarterly*, vol. 5.

Schauer, F. (1982) *Free Speech: a Philosophical Enquiry* (Cambridge University Press).

Schelling, T. C. (1984) *Choice and Consequence* (Harvard University Press).

Schneider, H. W. (1940) 'The Liberties of Man', in Anshen *Freedom, its Meaning*.

Schoultz, L. (1980) Book Review of Gastil *Freedom in the World*, in *Universal Human Rights*, vol. 2.

Scott, K. J. (1956) 'Liberty, Licence, and not being Free', in *Political Studies*, vol. 4.

—— (1959) 'Conditioning and Freedom', in *Australasian Journal of Philosophy*, vol. 37.

Scribner, P. H. (1972/3) 'Escape from Freedom and Dignity', in *Ethics*, vol. 83.

Scruton, R. (1983) 'Freedom and Custom', in Griffiths *Of Liberty*.

Sherover, C. (1984) 'The Temporality of the Common Good: Futurity and Freedom', in *Review of Metaphysics*, vol. 37.

Singer, M. G. (1970) 'Freedom from Reason', in *Philosophical Review*, vol. 79.

Singer, P. (1978) 'Rights and the Market', in Arthur, J. and Shaw, W. (eds) *Justice and Economic Distribution* (New Jersey: Prentice Hall).

Skinner, B. F. (1973) *Beyond Freedom and Dignity* (London: Penguin).

Skinner, Q. (1984) 'The Idea of Negative Liberty – Philosophical and Historical Perspectives', in Rorty, R. *et al.* (eds) *Philosophy in History* (Cambridge University Press).

Smith, G. W. (1977) 'Slavery, Contentment, and Social Freedom', in *Philosophical Quarterly*, vol. 27.

Somerville, J. (1962) 'Toward a Consistent Definition of Freedom and its Relation to Value', in Friedrich *Nomos IV Liberty*.

Spencer, H. (1851) *Social Statics* (London: Chapman).

Steiner, H. (1974) 'The Natural Right to Equal Freedom', in *Mind*, vol. 83.

—— (1974/5) 'Individual Liberty', in *Proceedings of the Aristotelian Society*, vol. 75.

—— (1980) 'Slavery, Socialism, and Private Property', in Pennock, J.R. and Chapman, J.W. (eds) *Nomos XXII Property* (New York University Press).

—— (1983) 'How Free: Computing Personal Liberty', in Griffiths *Of Liberty*.

Stephen, J. F. (1967) *Liberty, Equality, Fraternity* (Cambridge University Press).

Sterba, J. P. (1978) 'Neo-Libertarianism', in *American Philosophical Quarterly*, vol. 15.

—— and Kourany, J. A. (1980/1) 'How to Complete the Compatibilist Account of Free Action', in *Philosophy and Phenomenological Research*, vol. 41.

Strawson, G. (1986) 'On the Inevitability of Freedom (from the Compatibilist Point of View)', in *American Philosophical Quarterly*, vol. 23.

Swanton, C. (1979) 'The Concept of Overall Freedom', in *Australasian Journal of Philosophy*, vol. 57.

—— (1984/5) 'On the "Essential Contestedness" of Political Concepts', in *Ethics*, vol. 95.

Tawney, R. H. (1964) *Equality* (London: Unwin).

Taylor, C, (1979) 'What's Wrong with Negative Liberty', in Ryan *The Idea of Freedom*.

—— (1984) 'Kant's Theory of Freedom', in Pelczynski and Gray *Conceptions of Liberty in Political Philosophy*.

Taylor, M. (1982) *Community, Anarchy and Liberty* (Cambridge University Press).

Ten, C. L. (1980) *Mill on Liberty* (Oxford: Clarendon Press).

Thalberg, I. (1983) *Misconceptions of Mind and Freedom* (London: University Press of America).

Titmuss, R. M. (1970) *The Gift Relationship* (London: Allen and Unwin).

Vincent, J. (1987) 'Freedom and International Conflict: Another Look', in *International Studies Quarterly*, vol. 31.

Waldron, J. (1988) *The Right to Private Property* (Oxford:Clarendon Press).

Watson, G. (1982) (ed.) *Free Will* (Oxford University Press).

—— (1987) 'Free Action and Free Will', in *Mind*, vol. 96.

Weale, A. (1983a) *Political Theory and Social Policy* (London: Macmillan).

—— (1983b) 'Diversity and Toleration', in *Morrell Studies in Toleration*, (University of York).

Weinstein, W. L. (1965) 'The Concept of Liberty in 19th Century English Political Thought', in *Political Studies*, vol. 13.

Wertheimer, A. (1975) 'Social Theory and the Assessment of Social Freedom', in *Polity*, vol. 7.

White, D. M. (1969/70) 'Negative Liberty', in *Ethics*, vol. 80.

Wilson, J. (1958) 'Freedom and Compulsion', in *Mind*, vol. 67.

Young, R. (1980a) 'Autonomy and the "Inner Self"', in *American Philosophical Quarterly*, vol. 17.

—— (1980b) 'Autonomy and Socialisation', in *Mind*, vol. 89.

—— (1986) *Personal Autonomy: Beyond Negative and Positive Liberty* (London: Croom Helm).

Zimmerman, D. (1981a) 'Coercive Wage Offers', in *Philosophy and Public Affairs*, vol. 10.

—— (1981b) 'Hierarchical Motivation and Freedom of the Will', in *Pacific Philosophical Quarterly*, vol. 62.

Zimmerman, M. (1965/6) 'Is Free Will Incompatible with Determinism?', in *Philosophy and Phenomenological Research*, vol. 2.6

Index